M000311718

Published by: Plan Ahead Press
                      PlanAheadPress.com
To order additional copies: www.PsychotherapyTools.com

ISBN: 978-0-9913826-1-3
Library of Congress Number: 2015931412

Disclaimer and Terms of Use: The Author and Publisher have strived to be as accurate and complete as possible in the creation of this book. The Author and Publisher assumes no responsibility for errors, omissions, or contrary interpretation of the subject matter herein. Any perceived slights of specific persons, peoples, or organizations are unintentional. Names and identifying characteristics of individuals in this book have been changed.

The information provided in this book is for informational purposes only and is not intended as professional advice. Every effort has been made to ensure that the information contained in this book is complete and accurate. The author and publisher disclaim any responsibility for any liability, loss or risk incurred as a result, directly or indirectly, from the use of this book.

Please purchase only authorized editions of this book.

Printed in the USA

Acknowledgments

Thirty years ago I had the pleasure of coordinating the Self-Help Clearinghouse for the Mental Health Association in San Francisco, where we offered free consultation to local self-help groups. Since then, I have been fortunate to lead long-term therapy groups and teach other therapists about the joy of group work. I have witnessed the exchange of countless gifts. Groups truly are powerful sources of hope, support, strength, and resilience.

Every group session is a new adventure, filled with richness and learning for everyone involved.

I am indebted to countless group therapy patients, workshop attendees, students, and trainees for continually teaching me about the rich and healing power of group work. I could not have developed this manual without the sage advice, practical support, and encouragement of colleagues, family, and friends, especially Janet Hewins, Ph.D., Ann Williams, MFT, and the wonderful editorial and organizational skills of Elisabeth Tuck, Shendl Diamond, and Laura L. Russell.

Thanks!

Ann Steiner, Ph.D.
Ann Steiner, Ph.D., MFT, CGP, FAGPA

Table of Contents

Chapter 1: Welcome

Welcome to How to Create and Sustain Groups that Thrive

What group therapy leadership training did you have? If you are like most group therapists, you were lucky to have one class in graduate school and have had no supervision or training in how to create and maintain well-functioning, effective groups. The average participant in my workshops comes for precisely that reason. They learned how to do groups by the seat of their pants and are hungry for guidance. This manual is for all the dedicated group therapists and group leaders who have so much to offer, yet have not had the training, supervision, and the help needed to do the best they can for their groups. This manual is also for seasoned group psychotherapists who want to refine their screening and preparation systems. Each form is designed as a guide that you can modify for your groups.

Leading groups can be a rollercoaster ride, from the challenges of the planning stages, to the delight of adding the ideal new member to an ongoing group. Groups are rarely boring. Group leaders often have the joy of being an expert juggler, the gratification of a wise observer, and the pleasure of new learning.

The worksheets and forms are available as downloadable, interactive pdfs for your individual use. To order your downloadable copy, send an email to info@PlanAheadPress.com with "Worksheet PDF request" in the subject line. Please include your name, title, organization affiliation, if any, and approximate date you purchased your copy of "How to Create and Sustain Groups that Thrive."

I hope that this manual gives you the tools to find your own path to leading satisfying, growth inspiring and rewarding groups!

Ann Steiner, Ph.D., MFT, Certified Group Psychotherapist, Fellow: American Group Psychotherapy Association

Enjoy!

Chapter 2: Different Groups for Different Folks

The Healing Power of Group Work

A number of years ago I led an in-service training for the group therapy department in a local psychiatric hospital. The trainees were disillusioned by only being able to do what they referred to as short-term groups, where members sometimes attended as few as two times. These short-term groups consisted of what Donald Brown, M.D., a major contributor to the field, dubbed "flow-through groups." Membership in these groups changes constantly. Different members flow through each session. Each day, there were one or more new members, which made it a different group. This was especially challenging for the group leaders. The participants of the in-service training wondered how attending just a day or two of group sessions, with different members in each group, could be helpful. Drop-in crisis group leaders often face this challenge. Since they also do not get to witness member's progress, they too, rarely see the benefit of these super short-term groups.

As a group psychotherapist for over 30 years, screening hundreds of people for my more stable groups, I often hear that a positive group experience in a self-help or drop-in group, motivated the person to seek group therapy at a later time. This is the good news about the countless, often silent benefits of all kinds of group work.

When teaching trainees and students, I often describe the metamorphosis made by Chuck, a salesman who had an injury that made it impossible for him to work. Chuck became clinically depressed, stopped going out with friends, and withdrew from his family. His world became smaller and smaller. As a macho guy, Chuck had always prided himself on being independent and not asking for help. When he became suicidal, his pastor talked him into getting help at a psychiatric hospital.

After attending a few mandatory inpatient groups he began to feel less alone and started to feel that he might have something to offer others. He began to remember things that he enjoyed other than work, reconnected with a few friends, and started talking to some close family members. After he was discharged, his wife encouraged him to join a longer-term psychotherapy group.

When Chuck first started in my outpatient psychotherapy group, he couldn't answer questions about how he was feeling emotionally. He had never learned to identify his emotions. With the group's help, he grew to understand which situations he found upsetting and learned new ways to cope with them. During his first year in group, Chuck realized that not complaining or asking for help was getting in his way. With the group's help, he learned to plan a list of questions for his medical appointments, and other techniques for becoming a more active participant in his health care. As he came to terms with his disability, he began to talk more openly, not only in group but with family and friends. Within a year, Chuck and his wife had reconciled and he had become a valued, contributing member of the group.

He liked to regale new group members about how before he was hospitalized for almost killing himself and his wife, he wouldn't have been caught dead in any kind of therapy, much less a Bob Newhart therapy group.

Chuck left the hospital angry, still blame-shifting his anger to everyone including hospital staff. When I told some of Chuck's story during the in-service training years later, the director recognized the man I was referring to as one of the most difficult patients they had had in group - someone they had assumed would never seek treatment again unless the police brought him in.

A few years later, he referred to that hospitalization as the best thing that ever happened to him and attributed his experiences in group to having saved his life.

Chuck's story is a reminder that group members who have even one short, positive experience with group are likely to consider and benefit from this kind of support in the future. The short time Chuck spent on that locked ward, where he was required to attend group, helped him see that he didn't have to suffer alone or in silence. The interns who had known him during his hospitalization barely recognized the "rebuilt" group member they had had a hand in creating.

Types of Groups

What are the differences between self-help, support, psychoeducational, supportive/expressive, and psychotherapy groups?

Self-Help Groups

In self-help groups, membership is usually limited to one single common condition, illness, experience, heritage, shared interest or problem. The purpose of most self-help groups may be societal or personal change, or both. Some groups espouse specific ideologies for achieving change and others may aim to increase public awareness of the problem or illness, as seen with illness-related organizations and foundations. Self-help groups tend to be highly structured and task-oriented. Members often participate in order to change some aspect of themselves or their behavior. These groups combine support, education and mutual aid with an emphasis on being self-governing and self-regulating. Often, leaders are participants who share the group's issues.

Quilting bees, which date back to the 19th century, are often seen as the first informal self-help groups as they served two purposes: the first was to make the challenge of piecing together sections of each other's quilts easier. The second, less official function was to build community and support for women who often lived far apart and had few chances to socialize. Interestingly, Susan B. Anthony made her first speech advocating the vote for women at a quilting bee.

- Self-help groups usually follow a structure with members talking in turn. The format often discourages cross-talk (i.e., responding to each other during meetings). These groups may ask for small donations, but usually do not charge. Although a commitment to attend regularly is encouraged, participants are usually welcome to come without making an ongoing commitment. Members are also encouraged to be in contact with each other outside the group meetings. There is a wide range of different types of groups within this category. Some are highly structured, as in twelve-step programs and others may borrow from other kinds of groups.

Examples of these types of groups include: career or job transition groups, Grandparents Raising Grandchildren self-help groups, Alcoholics Anonymous, online support groups, etc.

Further Reading

Lieberman, M.A. (1990). A group therapist perspective on self-help groups. *International Journal of Group Psychotherapy,* 40(3), 251-278.

Lieberman, M.A. & Borman, L.D. (1979). *Self-help groups for coping with crisis: Origins members, processes, and impact.* San Francisco:Jossey-Bass.

Kurz, L.F. (1990a). The self-help movement: review of the past decade of research. *Social Work With Groups,* 13(3), 104-112.

Kurtz, L.F. (1997). Self-help and support groups: A handbook for practitioners. SAGE Publications, Inc., Thousand Oaks, CA.

Self-Help Clearinghouses

American Self-Help Clearinghouse: Telephone: (201) 625-7101 | TDD: (201) 625-7101

National Self-Help Clearinghouse: Telephone: (212) 354-8525

National Mental Health Consumers Self-Help Clearinghouse: Telephone: (800) 553-4539

Interest Groups

Many groups do not fall into the traditional categories described in this chapter. What I refer to as interest groups combine different features, definitions, structures, and boundaries of traditional groups. They are different in that they are not intended to be therapeutic. Instead, they address a wide range of interest areas or tasks such as political, work-related, hobby, or affinity. Some are professionally led, others use a structured self-help format with rotating leadership. Some charge fees, others invite donations to their group or organization.

Book clubs, writer's groups, and work-based groups are typical of interest groups. Some book clubs and writer's groups are highly structured with rules that discourage political and religious discussions. Others encourage wide-ranging discussions that use the book or sections of the book as jumping off points. Most interest groups have a particular approach, task or structure. They use different time commitments, including:

- Time-limited
- Time-limited, with an option to "re-contract"
- Commitment needed for a minimum number of meetings
- Some welcome members on a drop-in basis

Support Groups

Support groups are usually led by professionals and focus on one common problem, such as care giving, grief or bereavement groups. Some support groups may be led by caring volunteers, either within an agency, organizational setting or independent of any organization or affiliation. The primary purpose is usually to give emotional support and information. The duration may be long-or short-term and the membership may or may not have been screened. While many traditional support groups do not charge fees or collect dues, they are usually limited to a small group, and ask that members make a commitment to attend at least 4 sessions. Bereavement groups that are sponsored by a hospice agency, and led by professional staff, are a good example of support groups.

The themes and topics of self-help and support groups are often similar, leading to confusion about how these kinds of groups differ. In her book, *Self-Help and Support Groups: A Handbook for Practitioners*, Linda Farris Kurtz clarifies the distinctions between self-help and support groups and explains the differences between the wide range of groups within self-help and support groups. Both types of groups provide support and frequently include education. She points out that while both types of group help members achieve personal change, that support groups rarely focus on behavioral change or attempt to transform and reform members. Support group meetings are relatively unstructured, and are often led by professionals, with an emphasis on support.

Lieberman researched and wrote about the differences between theses 2 types of groups, emphasizing that support groups examine their internal processes by viewing the group as a "social microcosm." Other authors refer to this work as "process" or examining emotions and interactions that arise during group - in the moment. In contrast, by discouraging cross-talk during meetings, self-help groups keep the process from getting into territory best facilitated by trained clinicians. In doing so, self-help groups de-emphasize exploration of interactions in the moment, and do not rely on them as part of the therapeutic change process.

Another major distinction is the psychological distance and role differences between group members and the leader. Self-help group leaders are usually members as well as helpers, which limits the psychological distance. As in other professionally led groups, support group leaders maintain boundaries by not revealing their own problems, limit their contact between themselves and group members, and define their role as that of the expert.

The differences between support, supportive/expressive and psychotherapy groups is another source of confusion. One key difference is that support and supportive/expressive groups usually deemphasize the past, and focus instead on here and now experiences during group sessions. Although psychotherapy groups also explore members here and now experiences, the past may be related to current relationships both in and outside of the group. Over the past 10 years the difference between support groups and psychotherapy groups has become less clear. Some psychotherapists lead what they refer to as support groups, charge fees for their sessions, and view the group's task as primarily supportive as opposed to focusing on change.

For an overview of these distinctions, see the table, Major Differences Among Group Modalities, Chapter 2, page 18.

Further Reading

Cerel, J., Padgett, J.H., Reed, R.A. (2009). Support groups for suicide survivors: results of a survey of group leaders. *Suicide and Life-Threatening Behavior,* Vol. 39, No. 6, pp. 588-598.

Kurtz, L.F. (1997). Self-help and support groups: A handbook for practitioners. SAGE Publications, Inc., Thousand Oaks, CA.

Schloper. G. (1995). Expanding our view of support groups as open systems. *Social Work With Groups,* 18(1), 3-10.

Wilson, D. (2010). Reducing isolation: An adult cystic fibrosis support group sponsored by the University of Wisconsin Pulmonary and Critical Care Medicine. Retrieved from http://videos.med.wisc.edu/videos/1149.

Psychoeducational Groups

Many of these groups are structured like classes with time at the end of the meeting for discussion regarding a common illness, concern, or problem. The leaders may have (had) the problem or may be trained group leaders. The goal is to learn ways of coping with problems and to develop new skills, such as dealing with anger or diabetes. Most of these groups charge fees and ask that members commit to attend at least four sessions. These groups are usually time-limited, closed groups that include teaching information such as skill development and communication skills which are practiced in the group, as well as experiential sections that allow feedback, emotional expression, and discussion. Goals and activities are usually set by the leaders in advance, and some groups encourage members to support each other outside of the group. Other examples include Cognitive Behavioral Therapy groups for depression, and multi-family group work. Many of these groups follow a structured manual, including topics for each meeting.

Dr. Nina Brown has written what is considered a classic resource book, *Psychoeducational Groups: Process and Practice* (2011.) She starts with "the assumption that that these groups are provided for all ages and educational levels in practically every setting. Another basic assumption is that the groups emphasize education or learning rather than self-awareness and self-understanding. The cognitive component takes precedence over the affective component; indeed, for some groups the affective component may be completely absent…Such groups are used with children, adolescents, and adults in all kinds of settings, including hospitals, businesses, universities, governmental and social service agencies, and the military. They may consist of one session or many sessions.

Psychoeducational groups are a hybrid of an academic class and a counseling group and have many characteristics of each. They are like classes in which there are numerous participants, principles of instruction are applied, the presented material is intended to be learned and retained, and the leader is the expert/instructor" (page 8), Brown, N. (2011).

For helpful information about team development, classroom groups, group ice-breakers, diversity issues in groups, see Johnson and Johnson's *Joining Together*, listed below.

Greg Crosby, a pioneer in designing psychoeducational group programs points out that recent approaches such as "Cognitive Behavioral Therapy (CBT), Dialectical Behavioral Therapy (DBT), and Social Skills" groups fit under the category of psycho educational. Furthermore, he distinguishes between two types of psycho educational groups: "…dissemination of information only (orientation to therapy, orientation to depression, anxiety, schizophrenia, medication information) and dissemination of information and practice of skills for coping such as DBT, CBT, and Social Skills groups to thematic or focal populations" (Crosby, 2014).

Further Reading

Bieling, P., McCabe, R., & Anthony, M. (Eds.). (2006). Cognitive-behavioral therapy in groups. NY: Guilford Press.

Brown, N. (2011). Psychoeducational groups: Process and practice. Routledge, NY.

Crosby, G. & Altman, D. (2012). Integrative cognitive-behavioral group therapy. In J. Kleinberg (Ed.), Handbook of Group Psychotherapy. Malden, MA: Wiley.

Johnson, D. & Johnson, F. (2013). Joining together. (11th ed). Upper Saddle River NJ:Pearson.

MacKenzi, K.R. (1997). Time managed group psychotherapy: Effective clinical applications, *American Psychiatric Press*, NY.

Vacha-Haase, T., Ness, C., Dannison, L., & Smith, A. (2000). Grandparents raising grand-children: A psychoeducational group approach. *Journal for Specialists in Group Work*, 25(1), 67-78.

Supportive/Expressive Groups

Membership is usually limited to one common illness or problem such as cancer. Group leaders may be trained mental health professionals and/or, in some cases, cancer survivors. Some of these groups are short-term, manualized, time-limited groups, and others have no set ending date. There is sometimes a fee for these groups, although those held in hospital settings or cancer-based support centers are most often free to participants. Group discussions range from fears about upcoming treatment, sharing difficulties in asking for help as well as setting limits when needed, challenges related to medication and treatment, the development of coping mechanisms, talking about death and dying, redefining meaning, problem-solving, etc.

David Spiegel, M.D.'s pioneering work and research about the effectiveness of group therapy for breast cancer survivors is a classic example of this kind of group. In 1989 his powerful research findings were published in the *Lancet*. That article introduced a new kind of group therapy he called "supportive/ expressive" for women with metastatic breast cancer who participated in professionally led support groups. His landmark research showed that those who participated in the groups lived twice as long as those who did not participate in groups. Since his original studies, controversy has arisen about the magnitude of his results. Despite the controversy, there is general agreement among researchers and clinicians that this type of group significantly increases quality of life, and can contribute to longer life expectancy (Spiegel *et al.*, 1989).

This group approach combines education, support, and discussion. Members may or may not have been screened, and participants are most often encouraged to socialize and support each other outside of group.

Further Reading

Butler, L.D., Koopman, C., Neri, E., Giese-Davis, J., Palesh, O., Thorne-Yocam, K.A., Dimiceli, S., Chen, X., Fobair, P., Kraemer, H.C., & Spiegel, D. (2009). Effects of supportive-expressive group therapy on pain in women with metastatic breast cancer. *Health Psychology, 28*(5), 579-587.

Classen, C.C. & Spiegel, D. (2011). Supportive-expressive group psychotherapy, in Handbook of Psychotherapy in cancer care (eds M. Watson and D.W. Kissane), John Wiley & Sons, Ltd., Chichester, UK.

Spiegel, D. & Classen, C. (2000). Group therapy for cancer patients: A research-based handbook of psychosocial care. NY: Basic Books.

Walker, L.M., Bischoff, T.F., & Robinson, J.W. (2010). Supportive expressive group therapy for women with advanced ovarian cancer. *International Journal of Group Psychotherapy, 60,* (3), 407-427.

Psychotherapy Groups

Therapy groups provide a safe place to practice new ways of coping with old behaviors and talk openly about reactions that get in the way of effective communication. Professional psychotherapists design, screen, "match" and invite a small number, usually no more than 7 members who can relate to each other yet benefit from being in a heterogeneous group. Attending to, registering, and discussing one's emotional experience in the moment is a hallmark of this kind of group. Members are encouraged to talk about their most intimate thoughts, and to let the group know how they feel in the moment. Sharing their emotional experiences in the moment often leads to insight. Many psychotherapy groups explore how member's childhood histories effect their current life, emotions, and present day interactions in the group sessions. This contributes to more in-depth exploration and mutual understanding. Leaders are then enabled to interpret the group's process, and help members identify patterns that they want to modify. Process-focused groups help members learn more about their emotions and how others experience their behavior and its impact on others. These groups can be intense and are an investment in change. A long-term psychotherapy group offers a consistent, comfortable place to speak up, to help understand what is getting in the way of having more meaningful relationships, and to feel better about oneself. Most psychotherapy groups are led by licensed mental health providers who charge a fee, and hold the groups in their offices.

S.H. Foulkes, an English analyst in the 1940's, incorporated the Gestalt theory that the group is more than the sum of its parts, along with the view that group member's original group experience comes from their family of origin. His approach formed the cornerstone of group analysis, as distinct from group psychoanalysis. Regression and regressive transferences with the therapist were not encouraged. Instead, he viewed the group situation as "multipersonal," an opportunity for the analyst to emphasize the "here-and-now" experience of members. This perspective allows the group-analytic experience to be "corrective" - "ego training in action" (Foulkes and Anthony, 1965:52). Foulkes (1961) refers to groups as "halls of mirrors" - reminding us that groups can confront individuals with aspects of themselves they were previously unable to see.

The Handbook of Group Counseling and Psychotherapy, edited by Janice L. DeLucia-Waack, Cynthia R. Kalodnerm and Maria T. Riva (2013) is an excellent resource book. For example, their comprehensive chapter on multicultural and diverse counseling includes sections ranging from Group Work in Schools, to Gay, Lesbian, Bisexual and Transgender Clients, Queer, and Questioning Clients. Their updated version includes comprehensive sections regarding important focus topics and issues of interest to group therapists.

Yalom and Leszcz's classic, *The Theory and Practice of Group Psychotherapy* is worth reviewing periodically. Yalom's classic 11 therapeutic factors are especially helpful when describing the benefits of group treatment. Even seasoned group psychotherapists will benefit from the insightful, comprehensive chapters in Rutan, Stone, and Shay's 2014 edition of *Psychodynamic Group Psychotherapy.* This valuable resource book is also helpful in thinking about your group(s). Motherwell and Shay's book, *Complex Dilemmas in Group Therapy: Pathways to Resolution*, addresses theoretical issues, as well as common clinical dilemmas. The latter two books provide more detailed advice about dealing with the wide range of treatment populations and common challenges that arise when leading psychotherapy groups.

The selected references section at the end of this book includes a compilation of valuable articles that address important topics and different aspects of group work. The American Group Psychotherapy Association's International Journal of Group Psychotherapy is a rich resource, providing excellent in-depth articles about a wide range of group related topics.

Further Reading

DeLucia-Waack, J., Kalodner, C.R., & Riva, M.T. (Eds.). (2014). The handbook of group counseling and psychotherapy, Los Angeles, CA: Sage Publications.

Foulkes, S.H. (1961). Group process and the individual in the therapeutic group. *British Journal of Medical Psychology*, 34:23-31.

Foulkes, S.H. & Anthony, E.J. (1965). Group psychotherapy, the psychoanalytic approach. Karnac Books, London.

Motherwell, L. & Shay, J.J. (2014). Complex dilemmas in group therapy: Pathways to resolution. NY: Routledge.

Rutan, J.S., Stone, W.N., & Shay J.J. (2014). Psychodynamic group psychotherapy (5th ed). NY: Guilford.

Yalom, I.D. & Leszcz, M. (2005). The Theory and Practice of Group Psychotherapy (5th ed). NY: Basic Books.

Online or In Person?

Online groups are expanding, with new standards being created and changes happening rapidly.

Chat rooms, forums, discussion boards, and other forms of Internet communication offer ground-breaking changes for people who are physically isolated or have medical conditions that limit their ability to travel. These groups are attractive to people with shared medical problems, mental health issues, and life phase challenges.

Members of the armed services, patients who live in remote areas, or those who prefer to be anonymous may prefer an on-line group. Online groups are worth considering depending on the community served, practice setting and where patients live.

The title of Sherry Turkle's interesting and important book, *"Alone Together: Why We Expect More from Technology and Less from Each Other,"* describes one of our culture's largest challenges. She brings a broader perspective to her review of the history of the Internet and exploration of the numerous ways electronic devices are changing our lives. Her research includes conversations with the increasing number of people who prefer online relationships to in-person conversations. The challenges of "unplugging" from our devices is examined, while appreciating the advances made possible by easy access to helpful, at times life-saving information.

In *The paradox of internet groups: Alone in the presence of virtual others*, Haim Weinberg addresses the challenges and benefits of online groups, identifies the group leader's role as "forum manager" and emphasizes the importance of boundaries. Using a group analytic perspective, he explores issues of belonging, connection and other common issues seen in small, large, and the "worldwide group."

Barak and Grohol researched online mental health programs. In their study, they found that this alternative treatment model had the ability to reach more diverse populations, the advantage of convenience, and potential cost savings. Their review of the research literature showed great potential for computerized programs and online treatment for head injury patients, social phobia, depression and decision-making, and some alcohol related problems (Barak and Grohol, 2011). Clearly, further research is needed.

In their informative article about online groups for caregivers of people with a mental illness, Brian Perron *et al.*, refer to the option to "lurk" as an advantage for visitors to online groups. Perron points out that lurking allows one to observe the group without actively participating. "Many new participants prefaced their introductions with the fact that they had been lurking for a while. This introduced the participants to the norms and the issues typically discussed among group members. Lurking may reduce the attrition rate of participants." The authors recommend that therapists first lurk or vet on-line groups before recommending them. They suggest that the groups be screened for groups that are relevant to the caregiver's needs, have established norms for sending and receiving messages, and are accepting new members. They also advise that clinicians educate their clients about Netiquette, how to protect one's personal identity, and how the group can best meet their needs. The authors recommend that these groups be used as adjuncts to traditional groups.

When asked, I recommend in-person, face-to-face groups, whenever possible. The opportunities for learning and growth are dramatically expanded when nonverbal cues are accessible to the leader and group members. Un-moderated chat groups sometimes share misinformation. Nonprofessionals are more likely to miss signs that a member is suicidal or needs a higher level of care. Newly diagnosed medical patients, who often search the Internet for answers and cures, are especially vulnerable. These risks are heightened when there is no screening, which leads to mixing newly diagnosed patients with patients who have more end-stage disease. In-person group leaders can protect their members by keeping these groups separate. This reduces the risk of overloading or frightening newly diagnosed members. Protecting patients from these kinds of problems in the Wild West of the Internet is a major challenge.

As I tell my patients, Dr. Google did not go to medical school and cannot know your unique history and situation. When used as an adjunct to traditional group therapy I concur with Brian Perron, *et al.,* and recommend that the therapist be familiar with the norms, benefits and risks of online groups. This may involve lurking and checking out for yourself, the level of emotional safety and, quality of the advice given, any treatment recommendations etc.

On the plus side, responsible online forums, like the information exchange listserves mentioned later in the book in Chapter 8, can help patients and professionals keep current with recent literature and exchange ideas and different perspectives.

For an excellent overview of this burgeoning form of group work, see Betsy J. Page's chapter, *Online Group Counseling* (pages 609-620) in *The Handbook of Group Counseling and Psychotherapy,* edited by Janice L. DeLucia-Waack, Cynthia R. Kalodner and Maria T. Riva.

For more details about ways to keep online groups safe and for copies of online group agreements, see Chapter 8, page 67.

Further Reading about Online Group Work

Barak, A. & Grohol, J.M. (2011). Current and future trends in internet-supported mental health interventions. *Journal of Technology in Human Services*, 29(3):155-196.

Barak, A., Hen, L., Boniel-Nissim, M., & Shapira, N. (2008). A comprehensive review and a meta-analysis of the effectiveness of internet-based psychotherapeutic interventions. *Journal of Technology in Human Services*, 26:109-160.

Cohen, B.D. (2002). Group to resolve conflicts between groups: Diplomacy with a therapeutic dimension. *Group*, 26(3):189-204.

Davies, J. (2006). Hello, newbie! Big welcome hugs, hope U like it here as much as I do!: An Exploration of Teenagers Informal Online Learning. In: D. Buckingham & R.W. Mahwah (Eds), Digital Generations: *Children, Young People and New Media*. New Jersey and London: Lawrence Erlbaum, 211-229.

DeLucia-Waack, J., Kalodner, C.R., & Riva, M.T. (Eds.). (2014). The handbook of group counseling and psychotherapy, Los Angeles, CA: Sage Publications.

Kozlowski, K.A., Holmes, C.M. (2014). Experiences in online process groups: A qualitative study. *The Journal for Specialists in Group Work,* 39(4), 276-300.

Livingstone, S., Haddon, L. Gorzig, A., & Olafsson, K. (2011). Risks and safety on the internet: The perspective of European children. Full Findings. LSE, London. Online at www.eukidsonline.net.

Perron, B. (2002). Online support group for caregivers of people with a mental illness. *Psychiatric Rehabilitation Journal,* 26:70-71.

Polak, M. (2006). It's a URL thing: Community versus commodity in girl-focused netscape. In: D Buckingham & R.W. Mahwah (Eds.). *Digital Generations*: Children, Young People and New Media, 177-1973. NJ and London:Lawrence Erlbaum.

Turkle, S. (2011). Alone together: Why we expect more from technology and less from each other. NY: Basic Books.

Weinberg, H. (2014). The paradox of internet groups: Alone in the presence of virtual others. Karnac Books, London.

What Do These Groups Have In Common?

To recap, each of these types of groups can help members:

- Become more active participants in their emotional and physical health
- Reduce isolation
- Realize that they have perspectives and input of value to others
- Increase their sense of belonging and of having value to others
- Learn new coping tools
- Hear how others deal with similar problems, and discover healthier, more effective ways to cope

Time Commitments For Groups?

Short-Term Groups

Groups that meet for less than 8 sessions are generally thought of as short-term. Members are expected to make a commitment to come to each meeting. Some groups may continue beyond the set time period, while others may restart every few months. Short-term groups can be particularly helpful to the individual in crisis. This kind of group can give members a taste of what it is like to be in an ongoing therapy group. In addition, they can help members cope with immediate crises.

Drop-In Groups

In these groups, members don't need to make a commitment to attend. Participants are welcome whenever they want to come. The downside to drop-in groups is the possible loss of the comfort and trust created by meeting regularly with the same people.

There are times when a drop-in group is the best choice, especially when a person is in crisis. Participants may attend when they need support and benefit from knowing that help is available.

Long-Term Groups

These groups often have no pre-set ending date. Members usually leave this kind of group when they have made the interpersonal changes they wanted to achieve or have accomplished their initial goals.

Open versus Closed Groups

What is an Open Group?

Open groups accept new members during the life of the group. Examples include most twelve step groups, "Revolving Door" or Donald Brown's "T-Bag" groups in which members flow through, so that each session may have different members. Drop-in or crisis groups also fall into this category. The key feature is that while they are welcome to, group members are not expected to make a commitment to return.

What is a Closed Group?

Long-term psychodynamic psychotherapy groups are good examples of closed groups. In these groups, the membership remains stable until a member leaves or a new cycle begins. Groups which are designed to be short term, yet whose leader(s) offer to re-contract or start a new cycle, are considered "open" while new members are being accepted. Members are expected to make a commitment to attend regularly. Closed groups offer the advantage of continuity and the benefit of knowing that each member will continue in the group, which allows for greater intimacy and interactive risk-taking.

Ludwig von Bertalanffy was a pioneering biologist in the 1950's, who articulated and made connections between key concepts found in basic physics, chemistry, biology, and psychology, of special interest to family and group psychotherapists. He pointed out that conventional physics deals only with closed systems, i.e., systems which are considered to be isolated from their environment. His pioneering work underlies the foundation of systems theory, and most of the major theoretical approaches to group work. Many theoreticians also incorporate the impact of family and environment on group interactions and behavior patterns. One can use systems theory as a lens with which to view all interactions. What came to be known as general systems theory is based on von Bertalanffy's open systems theory (von Bertalanffy, 1966).

His writing has truly stood the test of time. If this intrigues you, I encourage you to read his 1969 book, *General System Theory: Foundations, Development, Applications*, George Braziller Inc.

The following table is designed to give an overview of the differences between the major types of group. When I first began working on this table with Donald Brown, M.D. in the 1980's there were only three categories to address. As the world of group work has expanded, I have added new categories to the table.

Major Differences Among Group Modalities

		Self Help	Interest Group	Psychoeducational	Supportive/ Expressive	Psychotherapy
1.	Motivation and Goals	Support and/or education. Lifestyle changes can be expected but not personality change. Want to learn new coping tools, increase self-understanding. Interpersonal problems not directly addressed.	Want to: Work on group project, share/exchange information and resources, contribute to community, learn new skills, knowledge, coping tools, increase self-understanding. Interpersonal problems sometimes explored - as they relate to improving self-care, problem-solving, and support.	Education, dissemination of information, emotional learning, and support. Want to learn new information, coping tools, increase self-understanding. Interpersonal problems addressed from a cognitive/experiential learning perspective.	Place to speak the unspeakable. Want to learn new coping tools, increase self-understanding. Interpersonal problems explored as they relate to improving self-care, problem-solving, and support.	Place to speak the unspeakable. "Risk taking" laboratory where interpersonal problems can be addressed. Want to change behavior, increase self-understanding.
2.	Leadership	Leadership by peers, leadership may rotate. Leaders guide structure for sessions.	Leader seen as discussion guide, instructor, facilitator, or coordinator.	Leader(s) are active and directive; seen as teacher/group-process oriented therapist/instructor. Leader outlines structure for each session.	Leader seen as therapist, expert, discussion guide, instructor, facilitator; not fellow sufferer.	Therapist seen as expert; not fellow sufferer.
3.	Focus on Past; Effect on Present	Past deemphasized.	Past rarely addressed, here and now experience explored in some groups.	Exploration of past discouraged, here and now. Past deemphasized.	Past often deemphasized, here and now experience often explored.	May address impact of past on present.
4.	Basic Rules, i.e., Time, Location, Fee	Rules set by group founders, as in AA, consensus or by dominant members. Fee rarely charged, donations sometimes requested.	Rules initially set by group instructor, revised with group input/consensus. Short-term format. Fees usually charged, unless waived for members of sponsoring organization.	Rules set by group therapist(s), may be revised with group input/consensus. Short-term format. Fee usually charged.	Rules set by group therapist(s), may be revised with group input/consensus. Short-term format. Fee usually charged.	Rules set by group therapist, revised with group input/consensus. Short-term or ongoing. Fee usually charged.
5.	Screening	May be no screening or follow-up.	May be no screening or follow-up.	Screening rarely occurs. Agency staff may triage, screen, match, and follow-up.	Therapist or agency staff usually responsible for screening, matching, and follow-up.	Therapist responsible for screening, matching, and follow-up.
6.	Group Composition	Usually defined and limited to common illness or problem.	Usually limited to common interest.	Usually limited to common illness or problem.	Usually limited to common illness or problem.	Mixture of diagnoses and problems possible.
7.	Outside Contact	Actively encouraged.	Usually supported.	Supported.	Supported or actively encouraged.	Discouraged. Discussion required when occurs.

Commonalities Among Group Modalities

1. All provide an antidote for isolation.

2. All increase the member's sense of belonging, and of having something of value to offer others.

3. All help manage stigma.

4. All help members learn new coping tools.

5. All help foster group problem-solving, helping member's increase their own problem-solving skills.

6. All help redefine life roles and priorities and to varying degrees explore identity issues.

7. All construct a new social network, either from the group itself or by encouraging acceptance of outside support.

8. All have a wide range of formats and follow different amounts of structure. Hybrid groups that draw from different approaches are increasingly common.

9. All can integrate patient education into their formats.

10. All can help members become more active participants in their emotional and physical healthcare. Groups organized around mental health and medical concerns can enhance a patient's understanding of their illness and increase self-care.

Screening and Follow-Up

Most participants in groups that are not led by mental health professionals are not screened. This means that the leader has not met or talked with members before they attend meetings. It can also mean that there is no plan for follow-up if and when a member is in crisis.

Structured self-help groups like Alcoholics Anonymous or Food Addicts Anonymous offer follow-up by encouraging members to have a sponsor who helps the sponsee learn about the program and deal with the challenges of their addiction. If the group is not a traditional twelve-step program, there may be a charge for the screening or preparation session. Some group therapists offer free evaluation and/or screening appointments. Many group leaders feel freer not to accept potential members into their groups because there is no charge for the screening session. I provide referrals when group candidates are not appropriate for my groups, and view these appointments as a consultation for which I charge. For more information and details about screening (see Chapter 4 with its Screening, Selection, and Preparation and Chapter 5, which includes sample screening protocols).

What Kind of Group to Recommend

Once a prospective member understands the different kinds of groups available, they usually know which type they want to pursue. For example, patients who are uncomfortable with the idea of talking to more than one person, often prefer starting with a less interactive group. They may be more comfortable in a psychoeducational group or a self-help group.

Deciding How You Want to Lead Your Group and Who You Want in it

Understanding the types of group leadership, formats, designs and structures available makes it easier to create and maintain the kind of group you want to lead. Being clear about the type of group(s) you lead will also help you describe and market your group. This, in turn will help you and potential group members decide whether your group is a good "fit."

Remember the phrase "works and plays well together"? If you are not a professionally trained group leader, how can you figure out whether the person who wants to join your group will benefit from and contribute to your group? How can you create and maintain a group where members feel emotionally safe, trusting, and find a sense of community? This book is designed to give you the tools to create and lead groups that offer members a sense of belonging and emotional safety.

As described in more detail in the following sections, having a clear idea of the group's purpose, what members can expect, and screening all help. When possible, screening/interviewing prospective group members is one of the most valuable tools in the group leader's toolkit. The most important information to learn about a group candidate is whether the person can be empathetic and supportive towards other group members. If members do not have basic social skills, empathy, or compassion at least for others if not themselves, those may be the very skills a different kind of group could help them learn. For example, domestic abusers and patients in crisis, while they may not fit in your long-term group, can benefit from a group designed to help them with their particular issues.

Reminder: The worksheets and forms are available as downloadable, interactive pdfs for your individual use. To order your downloadable copy send an email to info@PlanAheadPress.com with "Worksheet pdf request" in the subject line. Please include your name, title, organization affiliation, if any, and approximate date you purchased your copy of "How to Create and Sustain Groups that Thrive."

Types Of Groups: Worksheet

This worksheet is designed to help you clarify the format and design of your groups.

Suggestion: Check off any of the types of group that you lead or are planning.

Formats

☐ Manualized, i.e., different leaders can step in and continue following a standardized manual
☐ Structured
☐ Semi-structured
☐ Unstructured
☐ Psychodynamic, or other orientation with process focus

Time Frame Options

Short-Term vs. Long-Term

Reminder: Opinions differ about what comprises short- or long-term groups.

☐ Time-Limited
☐ Open versus Closed Groups, i.e., membership remains stable until a new cycle starts
☐ "Revolving Door" or Donald Brown, M.D.'s, flow-through groups, each session often has different members. For example, drop-in or crisis groups
☐ Waiting List Groups can allow leaders to diagnose and determine the best type of group for each member
☐ Re-Contract option offered for time-limited groups
☐ Traditional long-term groups, no ending date scheduled

Meeting Frequency

☐ Weekly, hour and a half
☐ Bi-weekly
☐ Monthly
☐ Bi-Monthly
☐ Other: Describe: _____

Setting: In-Person, Online, etc.

☐ In-person, church or library meeting room, office location, or member's homes
☐ Online structured, moderated
☐ Semi-structured
☐ Unstructured
☐ Other: Describe: _____

Leadership Structures

- ☐ Single leader
- ☐ Co-leadership especially helpful in self-help or groups led in training settings
- ☐ Rotating leadership, especially helpful for self-help or groups led in training institutions

Interest Groups

- ☐ Psychoeducational with a support or process section for discussion after didactic presentations
- ☐ Peer-led self-help/support groups
- ☐ Peer-led or professionally led writer's groups
- ☐ Peer-led book discussion groups
- ☐ Professionally-led self-help/support groups
- ☐ Supportive/Expressive groups
- ☐ Experiential Workshops
- ☐ Other: _____

Chapter 3: How to Plan a Group, The Nuts and Bolts

Identifying Your Leadership Style Worksheet

Directions: Check each leadership characteristic and tasks you are currently comfortable with. To use this as an ongoing tool, check items you want to add. Complete the form now, put it aside for a few months, then complete it again periodically.

NOW	DESIRED
Leadership Style	**Leadership Style**
☐ Active	☐ Active
☐ Blank screen	☐ Blank screen
☐ Compassionate	☐ Compassionate
☐ Confrontive	☐ Confrontive
☐ Didactic	☐ Didactic
☐ Directive	☐ Directive
☐ Empathic	☐ Empathic
☐ Neutral	☐ Neutral
☐ Passive	☐ Passive
☐ Transparent	☐ Transparent
☐ Warm	☐ Warm
☐ Other: _____	☐ Other: _____

Date Begun: _____   Date Revised: _____

The following section helps you clarify and focus on leadership tasks and roles that you are comfortable with and those that you would like to change.

NOW	**DESIRED**
Leadership Tasks/Roles	**Leadership Tasks/Roles**
☐ Boundary/limit-setter	☐ Boundary/limit-setter
☐ Cheerleader	☐ Cheerleader
☐ Choreographer	☐ Choreographer
☐ Coach	☐ Coach
☐ Consultant	☐ Consultant
☐ Director	☐ Director
☐ Facilitator	☐ Facilitator
☐ Frustrator	☐ Frustrator
☐ Gratifier	☐ Gratifier
☐ Group leader	☐ Group leader
☐ Guide	☐ Guide
☐ Head of marketing and recruitment	☐ Head of marketing and recruitment
☐ Interpretive guide	☐ Interpretive guide
☐ Motivator	☐ Motivator
☐ Prison guard	☐ Prison guard
☐ Role model	☐ Role model
☐ Structure designer	☐ Structure designer
☐ Survivor of similar difficulty to group	☐ Survivor of similar difficulty to group
☐ Resource guide	☐ Resource guide
☐ Teacher	☐ Teacher
☐ Team leader	☐ Team leader
☐ Traffic cop	☐ Traffic cop
☐ Treatment team collaborator	☐ Treatment team collaborator
☐ Treatment team coordinator	☐ Treatment team coordinator
☐ Treatment team leader	☐ Treatment team leader
☐ Other: _____	☐ Other: _____

Date Begun: _____   Date Revised: _____

Definitions of Leadership and Facilitation

Sometimes it helps to step back and look at the big picture. For example, it may help to review the actual definitions of facilitate and leader, that we assume we understand. Most will agree that facilitation is the main task or job title/description for a group leader. Webster's New Dictionary of the English Language, 1971, defines facilitate as "To make easy or less difficult." Here is the current Merriam-Webster definition: "one that facilitates; *especially*: one that helps to bring about an outcome (as learning, productivity, or communication) by providing indirect or unobtrusive assistance, guidance, or supervision "the workshop's *facilitator* kept discussion flowing smoothly."

The older version of Webster defines a leader as "one who or that which leads; a guide or conductor; a guiding or directing head, as of an army, party, movement; one for most or especially eminent in position, influence; conductor or director, as of an orchestra, band, or chorus: the player at the head of the first violins in an orchestra…"

Reminders for Leaders of New Groups

How you lead the first group session sets the tone for your new group. Gans, J. (1988) reminds us of the importance of encouraging discussion of the unconscious establishment of group norms in psychotherapy groups. Although these issues will be addressed in greater depth later, it is worth keeping in mind Gan's list of key leadership functions:

- Lateness and absence
- Leaving early
- Bringing food
- Tardy or unpaid bills
- Outside-of-group contact
- Breaches of confidentiality
- Termination

Further Reading

Caffaro, J.V., Conn-Caffaro, C., Sibling Dynamics, & Group Psychotherapy. (April 2003). *International Journal of Group Psychotherapy*, 53:125-154.

Gans, J. & Counselman, E. (2010). Patient selection for psychodynamic group psychotherapy: Practiceal and dynamic considerations. International Journal of Group Psychotherapy, 60(2), 196-220.

Rutan, J.S., Stone, W.N., & Shay J.J. (2014). Psychodynamic group psychotherapy (5th ed). NY: Guilford.

Yalom, I.D. & Leszcz, M. (2005). The theory and practice of group psychotherapy (5th ed). NY: Basic Books.

Action Plan for Starting New Groups

This next section addresses key steps that help you create and maintain cohesive and resilient groups. The worksheets are designed to help you plan and or refine ways to design or improve your current groups.

Step One: Investing the appropriate time to plan and design your new group is essential to making the group healthier and to your success in getting it started. This section provides suggestions about key issues to consider at this phase.

Step Two: Once you are clear about the type of group you will be offering, you will be ready to put your business person's hat on, and start marketing and recruiting appropriate members.

Step Three: Screen and prepare group members to enhance the health of your group.

Step Four: As you begin to plan your group, or consider adding new members, consider using any of the suggestions that fit your situation.

The following material will help you clarify goals for your groups and group design:

Group Structure and Design

What kind of group do you want to offer: self-help, interest group, supportive/expressive, psychoeducational, process-oriented, short- or long-term, open, or closed?

You may want to review the descriptions of the Major Differences Among Types of Group in the table on page 18.

Think about your leadership style, theoretical orientation, etc.

If you are a psychotherapist, are you a transference-oriented therapist? Do you track and attend to patient's projections, invite discussion of unconscious material, or use a cognitive behavioral model? Is your primary responsibility to facilitate and help group members stay with the agreed upon task, project or discussion? For details, see the "Identifying Your Leadership Style Worksheet" (page 23).

Planning Your Group: Worksheet

Check all that apply to your therapeutic orientation or leadership style:

- ☐ Psychodynamic, process-focused
- ☐ Cognitive behavioral
- ☐ Psychoeducational
- ☐ Supportive/Expressive
- ☐ Brainstorm Facilitator
- ☐ Other: Describe: _____

Who do you want to have in your group?

List your criteria for group membership: Target population, level of motivation, psychological mindedness, ability and willingness to agree to the group agreements, etc.

_____

_____

_____

Who do you want to rule out and/or refer elsewhere?

_____

_____

_____

_____

Do you want to lead a short- or long-term group?

- ☐   Short, time-limited group
- ☐   Short, time-limited group, that may re-contract to continue
- ☐   Open-ended, long-term group

Reminders: You and/or your group members may be more comfortable starting out as a short-term workshop or six session series. If members gel, click, or want to continue, you can always offer the option of what is called recontracting, which means that the group agrees to contract for a longer time frame. This can be an opportunity for group members to review their goals, discuss the group's purpose and decide on a time frame each member is comfortable committing to.

Effective group leaders set the tone, provide continuity, are responsive to the group's needs, and help create emotional safety. All groups benefit from periodically checking in with each other about whether members are getting their needs met–and discussing and agreeing to changes in the structure, format or group agreements. It is best to have these discussions during group meetings.

Marketing is not a One Time Project

You may wonder why recruitment and marketing are addressed in the section about planning your group. The short answers are: (1) Recruitment and marketing are usually the least favorite part of being a group psychotherapist. As a result, it is often the most overlooked aspect of the design and implementation phase; (2) Even closed, long-term psychodynamic groups have openings as people leave the group. Recruitment and marketing should be an ongoing process, not just when you are starting a new group.

For example, the next section about describing your group serves a dual purpose: helping you get clearer about who and what your group is for and what your group is about. The way you think about and how you describe your group is the first step in your marketing plan. Chapter 9 goes into more detail about marketing.

Choosing your words:

What you call your group, how you describe it, matters.

Your flier may be the first impression you give potential group members and referral sources. It is important to communicate clearly what your group does and doesn't offer. Consider creating your own focus group by having a few colleagues, as well as at least one person who is not a therapist, critique your flier.

An example of less inviting language for a group's name/description:

- Domestic Violence Group versus Self-Esteem Workshop, Class, or Group

Create your group description:

☐ Describe, in less than 100 words, your theoretical orientation
☐ Define, in less than 100 words, the group objectives
☐ Describe realistic expectations for potential group members
☐ Draft a short, inviting one-paragraph description of your group
☐ Practice reading each of these to at least one trusted colleague for honest feedback

Note for Work Group Leaders, etc.

Although you will not need all the detailed planning that follows, your groups will also benefit from having a group agreement as well as a form of agreement about termination. This can be either the kind of group termination agreement used in some traditional psychotherapy groups or a verbal agreement that members will say good-bye in person before leaving. IF appropriate, consider inviting group members to participate in open discussions about major decisions such as whether to rotate leadership, expectations of the leader, group agreements, and group format. Spelling out and occasionally reviewing with the group, the group's shared expectations increases cohesion, feelings of belonging and individual ownership.

Designing Group Agreements

As you think about the type of group you are creating or adding to, it will be helpful to review what you expect group members to commit to when they join your group.

Why provide a written group agreement for patients or group members to sign?

By writing out a list of agreements, group members become more active participants, share-holders as it were, of their group. Group agreements spell out basic ground rules that address physical and emotional safety. Often group agreements encourage open exploration of self-defeating behaviors and encourage open discussion of tough topics such as lateness. We cannot "legislate" and enforce these rules. Scott Rutan, Ph.D., a major contributor to the field of group therapy, suggests that group members take responsibility for their agreements without adhering to them blindly. Having explicit agreements sets the stage for the group to discuss more fully, problems that arise.

Instead of group agreements, many psychoeducational group leaders provide a schedule or agenda. Depending upon the population and topic, some may include written group agreements and office policies that explain confidentiality, discuss putting feelings into words not action, etc. Groups that encourage cross-talk and process often benefit from open discussion of these agreements which may lead to negotiated changes in the agreements. Samples of group agreements for different types of group are included in Chapter 7.

If You Don't Lead Psychotherapy Groups

Some non-profit groups and organizations who do weekend trainings using group formats, neglect to have participants sign an informal agreement that includes the basics like spelling out that this is not a therapy group and listing any group agreement/rules. Often these less formal groups overlook either requesting or requiring that participants give them information about their emergency contact person. Having this information and when appropriate, essential medication information can be life-saving.

Depending on the type and purpose of your group work, consider inviting group members to participate in open discussions about major decisions such as expectations of the leader, the group itself, group agreements, and group format. Groups led in work settings have different dynamics and challenges than the other groups discussed thus far. The key difference is that group participation may not be optional, and the leader may have the dual role of being both the boss and the group leader, which can inhibit free expression among group members. In some cases employee's participation may be reflected in performance reviews and evaluations. Also, depending on the work or corporate culture there may or may not be a value placed and put into action, of collaboration, and the free expression of ideas. Small computer start-up companies tend to be more similar to the kinds of groups described in this book. For example, group or team leaders in their work settings are likely to benefit from spelling out and occasionally reviewing with the group, it's objectives. Generally speaking, when the culture makes it safe, open discussion of group expectations increases cohesion and creativity.

The next page has a sample of a basic psychotherapy group agreement. Feel free to modify or have your group participate in modifying the agreement:

Sample Basic Psychotherapy Group Agreement

YOUR LETTERHEAD HERE

<u>Your name</u>
<u>Your Office Address</u>
<u>Your Phone Number</u>
<u>Your email address</u>

Group Agreements

As a group member I agree to the following:

1. To be present each week, to be on time, and to remain throughout the meeting.

2. To give the group as much notice as possible of any planned absences.

3. To work actively on the problems and issues that brought me to group.

4. To put my feelings into words, not actions.

5. To use the relationships made in the group therapeutically, not socially.

6. To reduce secrecy and keep discussions open, I will let the group know about outside group contacts.

7. To remain in the group until I have met my goals and/or the problems that brought me to group have been resolved.

8. To follow the group termination guidelines I have agreed to.

9. To be responsible for my bills, to pay them promptly, and discuss, in group any questions about my bill. To pay for any missed sessions that are not due to illness or unavoidable emergencies and to discuss any concerns or conflicts that may arise over the fee.

10. To protect the names and identities of my fellow group members

Signature: _____

Date: _____

Copy Received: ☐ Yes ☐ No

Note: Adapted with permission from Rutan, J.S., Stone, W.N., & Shay J.J. (2014). Psychodynamic group psychotherapy (5th ed). NY:Guilford.

Contact between Group Members Outside of Group

In reviewing or designing your group, it helps to clarify your expectations about what is referred to as outside-of-group contact, i.e., members connecting with each other socially, via phone or online contact, etc.

Traditional psychodynamic groups discourage members from socializing or being in contact with each other outside of the group's meeting time. Psychotherapy groups are seen as a place to learn about oneself in relation to others, as opposed to being a place to meet new friends. Followers of Yalom emphasize his description of group as a laboratory in which one can observe and learn from interactions, the benefits of which are diluted when the boundaries become permeable. As with traditional psychodynamic agreements about outside of group contact, the negative effects include the risk of splitting, conflicts arising that cannot be addressed in the group, members feeling left out, etc.

Other types of therapy groups and leaders encourage the use of outside-of-group contact even for traditional psychotherapy groups. While this choice can be controversial, this adjunct to in-person meetings is growing in popularity. If you decide to endorse or encourage this kind of contact, it is important for the group to understand and agree about the purpose, risks, and potential complications that can arise as a result of outside of group contact. Depending on your perspective, online or other personal contact between sessions can increase members feeling of belonging and connection. Most psychoeducational group leaders focus on the potential benefits of increased connections for isolated individuals.

When an outside of group contact agreement is agreed upon, it helps if members commit to letting the group know about the contact(s), agree to discuss in group, any conflicts or issues that arise in that contact, and for the leader to encourage group members to discuss their feelings about the contacts occurring outside of group sessions. Often the group will agree not to discuss what goes on in group with each other outside of group, and to bring any such discussion back into the group. In short, all such contacts must be discussable in group. Similar issues arise with social, phone, texting, and online contact between groups members.

In the 1960's a different version of outside-of-group contact in psychotherapy groups was initiated by some group leaders who would mail, using snail mail, a summary of the last group session. Some groups have adapted this practice on the Internet as a way of maintaining connection and keeping members who are unable to attend in person in the loop. Yet other groups have members take turns writing these summary notes. Although this adds another layer of complexity some leaders find that it helps group members maintain their feeling of connection. Naturally, in a therapy group, this becomes further grist for the mill. Given that the Internet is not private, it is important for all members to be reminded of this limitation and to be comfortable with this non-traditional method. When this outside-of-group process is endorsed by the leaders, it is important that its use and limitations be part of the group agreement members sign at the outset.

My personal policy with my traditional psychotherapy groups, is to discourage outside of group contact including online, especially any sharing of personal and/or private information. Clearly, this cannot be enforced. Instead, to reduce splitting and potential negative effects, members agree to let the group know about the nature of the contact, to avoid inviting or holding secrets about the contact, and agree to discuss any issues that the contact may create. A few of my groups negotiated their wish to be in contact with each other between sessions, made agreements for how to minimize the complications already discussed, and talk openly about these contacts in group when they become complex. Here, as in other situations, members of my long-term process-focused groups find open negotiations to modify the original group agreements to be beneficial and therapeutic.

The key to dealing with the question of outside-of group-contact effectively lies in the leader's maintaining the boundaries that define the group. In traditional psychotherapy groups this requires understanding the complexities that can arise for the group itself and each group member, the need for the leader to be consistent and encourage the group to talk about feelings that come up in response to the outside of group contact agreement. Nevertheless, I recommend that this kind of contact be kept to a minimum to protect the group boundaries and minimize misunderstandings. Whichever policy you decide to put in place for your group, it is important to raise the topic periodically to check in about how it is working. The section, Chapter 8, Internet Contact between Group Members about online group agreements (page 67) goes into detail about different ways to help online groups maintain a sense of safety and connectedness.

Congratulations on taking the time to plan your group. Completing this work is one of the most often overlooked steps to creating groups that thrive!

The next step is to decide what kind of screening, selection and preparation of group members will work best for your group.

Chapter 4: Screening, Selection, and Preparation

Screening System/Selection

Nathan HarPaz addresses the importance of screening for psychotherapy groups succinctly in his excellent article, *"Failures in Group Psychotherapy: The Therapist Variable"* (1994). He wrote, "Without a growing, real relationship to anchor the patient while still in the initial phase, he or she will not be able to tolerate the stormy, affect-laden group psychotherapy process."

The other major benefit to doing one's own screening and preparation of group members is that it allows you to: assess readiness for your particular group, formulate diagnostic impressions, get a flavor of the transference, level of connectedness, capacity for empathy, etc. Beyond helping you determine whether a candidate is appropriate for your group, screening makes it possible to match people across several dimensions that are beyond the scope of the present overview.

Benefits of comprehensive screening include assessing the following key dimensions:

- Ability to experience and reflect on interactions both in and out of group
- Capacity for empathy and attachment styles
- Capacity to acknowledge the need for others
- Capacity to work effectively within organizations and social situations

Phase One – Screening

My screening and preparation system for creating and adding members to my psychodynamic therapy groups is collaborative. By collaborative, I mean that I am open and direct as we think through together whether and how the type of therapy group we are considering is likely to be a good fit. I find it essential to meet individually with each person for 3 or 4 sessions, depending on whether they have been in therapy or other groups before.

Over the years, patients have found that the forms I have developed help them think through what they want out of a therapy group. They help us focus on the patient's issues and decide whether he or she is likely to benefit from and contribute to the group. In this way, new members feel more connected to the group process and the groups have significantly less turnover.

A number of years ago, I reluctantly experimented with the addition of a Group Life History form, (Chapter 6, page 44) which I email to patients so they can fill it out in advance and bring to our first session. As you will see, the form is designed to help group therapy candidates review their past experiences in group and begin to think more clearly about what they want from group at this time. Invariably, the response is one of appreciation for how seriously I take their needs and the screening process.

During the first session, I skim over their responses, asking how it felt to fill out the form, and we are off to a good start. The first appointment allows us to see whether we can work well together. If we agree that he or she is likely to benefit from and be able to contribute to one of my groups, I describe what we will use the next sessions to address. I also ask patients to sign a Release of Information form, giving me permission to talk with their individual therapist, psychiatrist or other providers they want me to collaborate with. In the section that describes the kind of information desired I write "treatment planning, history and coordination." Speaking with prior or current therapists often gives useful information, including whether the therapist or provider is supportive of the patient joining a group. At the end of this first session, I give them a copy of the American Group Psychotherapy Association's pamphlet "*Why Group*" to review before we meet again. In the following sessions, we work together to list the person's group goals as distinct from goals they may have for individual therapy. We then begin to discuss the challenges that may arise and, as discussed in the section on this topic, in this chapter (page 36) prepare the patient for joining the group.

Creating Individualized Group Goals

Since I was trained to take verbatim process notes, I have incorporated my laptop into my screening/intake process. During the one-on-one sessions, I take notes and insert an asterisk whenever I hear something that might be a good phrase or content area to include in their goals. Following the second or third session, I review my notes, hit Control F (the computer's Find function) to find the asterisks and put together the first draft of the person's group goals. We then review and edit these goals together. The end result is a one-page list that includes realistic, measurable changes in behavior or feelings, along with general areas to be addressed for group input and/or support.

Important Reminder – Screening/Intake Often Feels Like a Job Interview

Many of us forget how anxiety-provoking it is to join a new group. We also tend to forget that routine screening appointments are often experienced as though they are job interviews. The fear of rejection, while frequently disguised so as to make a good impression, should not be underestimated. This is another reason many therapists offer their initial intake/screening session free of charge or offer a half hour consultation.

When Screening Is Not an Option Where You Work

Not all group therapists have the luxury of meeting with group candidates even once, much less 3 or 4 times. Clinicians in agency settings often have no input as to who is put in their groups. Their interventions and treatment planning can still benefit from screening – a different kind of screening. Screening may not be needed in the group(s) your lead. For example, since they are not doing psychotherapy, work group leaders, interest group and other facilitators rarely feel the need to screen group members. If you are leading a group in which emotions or reactions that cannot be dealt with in the group may come up, be sure to have a current list of trusted referral sources, psychotherapists who have experience working with similar issues, as well as phone numbers for the local crisis line and referral services in your community.

Screening on the Fly

Ongoing and long term psychotherapy groups give leaders the opportunity to get to know the members and what they need from group. When you don't have the option of screening group members, there is a wealth of data you can put together over time. The key source is your observation of each member's relational and defensive styles. By observing and listening to the material and emotions shared, you can put together a working diagnosis. Your ideas of possible diagnoses and personality traits can, for example, inform how and whether you push or challenge a group member.

Phase Two – Selection

Selecting patients that you think will benefit and complement other group members is challenging - especially for therapists new to leading groups. It helps to review your group description and what the group is designed to offer group members. When selecting group candidates it also helps to review the impact of one's counterference reactions to both the group's needs and group candidates. Before accepting new members, step back and check in about your motivations. Make sure that the decision to add a new member is not unduly influenced by either financial pressures or because the group needs new members. If you are feeling desperate for new members – think twice. Make sure you are not risking adding a member who will is unlikely to be a good addition to the group.

When selecting members, it is best to choose individuals who are similar in terms of ego development, but different in terms of interpersonal style. Also, group members benefit more when they have members who are homogenous in the level of psychopathology, but heterogeneous in their personality type and presentation of problems.

Screening/Selecting Out

Sometimes, patients need our help to consider a group other than the one we were considering. For example, it may help to recommend a more structured, twelve-step program, a DBT group, or a crisis-focused group. By starting out in either a peer-led, time-limited highly structured, or drop-in group, many patients are better able in the future, to benefit from a process-focused psychodynamic group.

Saying "No" to group candidates can be one of the most challenging tasks for group leaders. The fear of rejecting and hurting patients who are not a good fit with an existing group often unduly influences therapists who later regret their decision. Adding inappropriate members can have long-ranging negative effects for the patient and the group. Sometimes the best help we can offer is our professional opinion that this group is not likely to be helpful and that another type of group would be better. Remember to have current contact information and phone numbers for your local community resources, e.g., crisis services, domestic violence hot-lines, drug and alcohol treatment, and psychiatric hospitalization facilities.

Following is a list of common grounds for exclusion from heterogeneous groups. Interestingly, there are groups that can be beneficial for each category.

Possible reasons to exclude a potential group member include:

☐   In acute crisis
☐   Imminently suicidal
☐   Insufficient impulse control
☐   Chronically psychotic
☐   Sociopathic
☐   Organic brain disorders
☐   Unable to commit to attend consistently

Most of the above are excluded since they are unable to establish the minimal object relatedness required for traditional group psychotherapy to work effectively.

Phase Three – Preparation/Orientation

In the final preparation/orientation session, the group leader allows time to encourage the incoming member to focus more directly on concerns about starting group, finalize goals, and discuss the group and termination agreement (templates in Chapter 7). Yalom (2005), found that one of the most significant reasons for early departures was inadequate orientation to group therapy.

During this final phase, I review and discuss the Group Agreements and the Termination Agreement form, which I have patients sign. They too, keep a copy of these agreements for their files along with their Group Goals.

Termination: Overview

Why Have a Written Termination Agreement?

Termination is the richest, most important, and challenging phase of treatment.

Leaving group with a feeling of accomplishment instead of in anger is, for many, a sign of major growth. Having an explicit termination agreement helps groups deal with important termination work.

The end of this chapter includes is a copy of the termination agreement I have designed and use with all my groups. Although group members frequently don't recall having been asked to read and sign the agreement during the intake process, many members find it helpful to have the explanation written out.

In his survey about whether group therapists talk about termination during their pre-group preparation sessions, Mangione *et al.,* found that 59% did discuss expectations about termination during their pre-group preparation sessions. He concluded that "Explicit preparation including discussion of endings, is crucial to ending well in groups and reflects the ethical value of autonomy" [Mangione, L.,

Rosalind F.R., & Iacuzzi, C.M., (2007). Ethics and endings in group psychotherapy: Saying good-bye and saying it well. *International Journal of Group Psychotherapy*, 57(1), p. 35)]. Chapter 7 has a sample termination agreement and includes a discussion about different kinds of termination.

As described in Chapter 10, the termination phase of group work can be the most important, healing, yet challenging phase of psychotherapy.

All groups, by their very nature, have the potential of being therapeutic. Many cohesive groups are therapeutic - without being therapy. The best group therapists and group leaders, tell their participants at the outset that the work they will be doing is likely to stir up strong emotions, which may not be able to be dealt with fully in the group. Non-psychotherapy group leaders make it clear that the group is not intended to either be or replace psychotherapy. Group members usually feel protected when the leader reminds them about these limits.

Depending on your treatment population, you may need to focus on different areas of emphasis during the screening and preparation process. If, for example, you work with patients with medical illness, I recommend that you avoid mixing patients with terminal illness and those who have chronic medical illness. When dealing with life-altering medical illnesses, it is usually wiser to have separate groups for the Newly Diagnosed and for Care-Partners. Whenever possible, it helps to hold these groups at the same time and location.

Starting New Groups – Balancing Acts

One of the biggest obstacles to starting groups is maintaining the interest of patients who are ready to start while you are still recruiting and screening others. The waiting period for those who are ready to start and for the group leader is anxiety-provoking. The reality is that referrals trickle in and are outside of our control. We need to help patients who are "on hold" stay connected and optimistic about starting the group. This is no small feat.

This limbo period of putting together a new group can lead to the therapist feeling desperate and accepting members we might not if we weren't feeling pressured. As Gans and Counselman (2010) remind us, we need to be mindful of and combat our countertransference and financial needs. It is important to check in with ourselves periodically to make sure that our decisions are not being unduly influenced by financial pressures.

Another antidote to these two common pitfalls is to make it clear to each accepted group member that the target start date will likely change, depending on when there are enough members to start the group. You can offer to keep them posted as often as they would like. Most prefer to be kept posted every few weeks and to be given at least a week's notice about the start date.

Reminder for First Sessions of New Groups

The first group session sets the tone for your new group. Gans, J. (1988) reminds us of the importance of encouraging discussion of the unconscious establishment of group norms. He refers to the following list as key leadership functions:

- Lateness and Absence
- Leaving early
- Bringing food
- Tardy or unpaid bills
- Outside-of-group contact
- Breaches of confidentiality
- Termination

The next chapter includes several Screening Protocols, the Group/Life History Questionnaire, a sample office policy, a Termination Agreement, and sample group agreements.

Congratulate yourself on having gotten this far!

Starting a new group, coordinating schedules, and finding appropriate group members who can contribute to and benefit from being in a group together is no simple feat. This is an accomplishment worth celebrating!

ENJOY!!

Recommended Reading

Bernard, H.S. (1989). Guidelines to minimize premature terminations. *International Journal of Group Psychotherapy*, 39, 523-529.

Gans, J. & Counselman, E. (2010). Patient selection for psychodynamic group psychotherapy: Practical and dynamic considerations. *International Journal of Group Psychotherapy*, 60(2), 19-220.

HarPaz, N. (1994). Failures in group psychotherapy: The therapist variable. *International Journal of Group Psychotherapy*, 44(1), 3-21.

Hoffman, L. (1999). Preparing the patient for group psychotherapy. Academic Press, London. 25-43.

Mangione, L., Rosalind F.R., & Iacuzzi, C.M. (2007). Ethics and endings in group psychotherapy: Saying good-bye and saying it well. *International Journal of Group Psychotherapy*, 57(1), p. 35.

Motherwell, L. (2011). Support and process-oriented therapy groups. The Wiley-Blackwell Handbook of Group Psychotherapy. John Wiley & Sons, Ltd., Chichester, UK, 275-298.

Ormont, L. (1957). Preparation of patients for group psychoanalysis. *American Journal of Psychotherapy*, 9, 841-848.

Ormont, L. (1969). Group resistance and the therapeutic contract. *International Journal of Group Psychothotherapy*, 18, 147-154.

Ormont, L. (1990). The craft of bridging. *International Journal of Group Psychotherapy*, 40, 3-17.

Piper, W.E. & McCallum, M. (1994). Selection of patients for group interventions. In H.S. Bernard and K.R. Mackenzie (Eds.). *Basics of Group Psychotherapy,* 1-34. NY: Guilford.

Price, J.R., Hescheles, D.R., Price, & Rae, A. (1999) (eds). A guide to starting psychotherapy groups. Academic Press, London.

Rutan, J.S., Stone, W.N., & Shay J. (2014). Psychodynamic group psychotherapy, (5th ed). NY: Guilford Press.

Toseland, R.W. & Siporin, M. (1986). When to recommend group treatment: A review of the clinical and group literature. *International Journal of Group Psychotherapy*, 36, 171-201.

Yalom, I.D. & Leszcz, M. (2005). *The theory and practice of group psychotherapy*, (5th ed). NY: Basic Books.

Chapter 5: Screening Protocols

As described earlier, screening is one of the key ways to create and maintain groups that thrive. These sample protocols for psychotherapy groups can help you think through and decide what information will help you assess whether each group candidate is likely to be a good match for your group.

Screening Protocol for General Therapy Groups

I.   DIAGNOSTIC IMPRESSION

      A.   Form diagnostic impression using all DSM - V Axes
      B.   Assess:
          1.   Crisis level
          2.   Suicidality, past and present
          3.   Substance use, abuse, past and present
          4.   Violence potential and history
          5.   Psychiatric hospitalization(s)
          6.   Level of impulse control
          7.   Coping strengths and awareness of these strengths
          8.   Quality of relationships, attachment history, and style

II.   HISTORY

      A.   Brief medical history, medical hospitalization history, list of medications
      B.   Brief family history of psychiatric and or substance abuse disorders
      C.   History of individual therapy, approximate dates and duration of treatment episodes
      D.   Nature, quality, and impact on treatment of transference

III. HISTORY OF GROUP EXPERIENCE

      A.   History and experience of self-help, and or therapy group participation
      B.   Overview of experience with family of origin, sense of belonging and connectedness
      C.   Religious upbringing, current involvement with church or spiritual group

IV.   ASSESSMENT OF GROUP HISTORY

      A.   Assess characteristic patterns of:
          1.   Entering
          2.   Dealing with
          3.   Participating in
          4.   Coping with conflict
          5.   Leaving groups
      B.   Characteristic roles taken in group settings

V.   <u>GROUP EVALUATION</u>: Assess the following:

    A.   Capacity for empathy
    B.   Level of motivation to change
    C.   Receptivity to and ability to use feedback
    D.   Capacity for empathy, identification with others
    E.   Capacity to acknowledge need for others
    F.   Extent of anger, and characteristic method of expressing hostility
    G.   History of conflict avoidance
    H.   Ability to maintain emotional equilibrium when others are in acute
        distress
    I.   Capacity for insight, to experience and reflect on interactions
    J.   Expectations re how group will be helpful, realistic?
    K.   Preferred styles of eliciting and receiving help
    L.   History of capacity to work effectively within organizations and social settings
    M.   Capacity to make and keep commitments

Screening Protocol for Chronic Medical Illness Groups

Diagnostic Impression

I.   DIAGNOSTIC IMPRESSION

    A. Form diagnostic _impression_ using all DSM V Axes
    B. Assess crisis level:
        1. Crisis level
        2. Suicidality, past and present
        3. Substance use, abuse, past and present
        4. Violence potential and history
        5. Psychiatric hospitalization(s)
        6. Level of impulse control
        7. Coping strengths and awareness of these strengths
        8. Quality of relationships
        9. Potential for and history of violence in living environment

II. HISTORY OF TREATMENT

    A. History and experience of treatment, self-help, and or therapy group participation
    B. Overview of experience with family of origin, responses to diagnosis and chronicity
    C. Religious/ spiritual upbringing, values, current involvement with church or spiritual group
        1. Explanation of illness, disability, limitation(s) as understood
        2. Assess level of motivation to change, beliefs about capacity for change, etc.
        3. Assess ability to identify and express both physical and emotional needs
        4. Assess extent of anger, and characteristic method of expressing "negative emotions"
        5. Assess capacity for insight, to experience and reflect on interactions
        6. Assess expectations re how treatment will be helpful
        7. Assess customary style of eliciting and receiving help
        8. Assess capacity to work effectively within organizations and social settings

III. ASSESSMENT OF RESPONSE TO MEDICAL DIAGNOSIS

    A. Length of time "receiving" diagnosis, amount of trauma involved
    B. Newly diagnosed, length of onset and progression of disease
    C. Level and type of involvement and participation in medical care
    D. Knowledge and ability to explain illness, prognosis, medications, side-effects etc.
    E. Impact on self-image, identity, experience of self-efficacy, social role

IV. ASSESSMENT OF ATTITUDE TOWARDS ILLNESS/ DISABILITY

    A. Level of understanding of diagnosis, prognosis, treatment options, etc.
    B. Familiarity, or lack of familiarity with implications for lifestyle and ways to maximize health and independence
    C. Beliefs and comfort re: complaining, asking for help, etc.
    D. Characteristic emotional and learning style, response style available to help patient metabolize, integrate lifestyle changes, future planning, etc.

V.   <u>TRAUMA HISTORY</u>

    A. Assess history of prior trauma, family of origins reactions
    B. Assess patient's <u>characteristic</u> patterns of responding to:
       1. Emotional pain, losses
       2. Physical pain
       3. Conflict in past and current responses to challenges experienced with significant others and medical team/systems

Chapter 6: Group/List History Form

What follows is a copy of the Group/Life History Form that I have all prospective group members complete and bring with them to our initial screening session. This form is designed as a template. It is not intended to fit every clinician's specific practice. Although the level of detail invited in this form is not appropriate for many of the groups discussed in this book, the following section is included to give readers an idea of the kinds of questions discussed during screening and preparation sessions for traditional psychotherapy groups. *Please adapt the form to meet your particular needs.*

YOUR LETTERHEAD HERE

Group/Life History Questionnaire

The purpose of this questionnaire is to put together a picture of your history and background. By answering these questions as fully and accurately as you can, you will facilitate your therapy. Completing this form will also save the time and expense of collecting this information during your session. If you need more space for ANY of the questions, please use the back of the page. If you do not wish to answer any questions, feel free to skip them.

This information will be kept strictly confidential. As described in my office policies, no outsider, not even your closest relative or family doctor, is permitted to see your case record without your written permission.

General Information *(Feel free to take as much space as needed)*

Date: _____   Age: _____   Gender: _____

Name: _____   Date of Birth: _____   Work Phone: _____

Address: _____   Home Phone: _____   Cell Phone: _____

Private messages may be left at which phone?   _____

With whom are you now living?   _____

Occupation: _____

Racial Identity
☐ African American   ☐ Native American   ☐ Euro-American
☐ Latina/o   ☐ Middle Eastern   ☐ Pacific Islander   ☐ Other

Clinical

What brings you to therapy? List your chief complaints/symptoms or issues you want to work on in group:

_____

_____

_____

What challenges would you like to deal with or what do you want out of a group?

_____

_____

_____

Give a brief history of the above, from onset to present:

_____

_____

_____

Have you been in outpatient therapy before? (If yes, when, how long, with whom?)

_____

_____

_____

Have you had any psychiatric hospitalizations? (If yes, when, where, for how long, diagnosis)

_____

_____

_____

Current psychiatric medications: (Please also fill out the Medical Information Form from www.DrSteiner.com for a more complete list of medications):

_____

_____

_____

Previous psychiatric medications:

_____

_____

_____

Family psychiatric history:

_____

_____

_____

Current/past use of drugs or alcohol? Please specify:

Substance	Amount and Frequency	First Use/Last Use

Do you smoke?   How much?   If former smoker, when did you quit?

☐ Yes   ☐ No   _____   _____

Major illnesses or operations?

_____

_____

_____

Current medications: (If not already completed, please also fill out the Medical Information Form from http://drsteiner.com/medform_intro.html for a more complete list of medications):

_____

_____

_____

When was your last complete physical exam?

_____

Results?

_____

_____

Sleep average hours per night?   _____   Insomnia?   _____

Recent appetite: ☐ Poor   ☐ Average   ☐ High

History of eating disorders? Anorexia, bulimia, binging/purging?

_____

_____

_____

Present height? _____   Present weight? _____

How much weight have you gained/lost in the last year? _____

Average exercise per week? _____

When was the last time you felt well both physically and emotionally for a sustained period?

_____

Present interests: _____

How is most of your free time occupied?

_____

Do you make friends easily? _____ Do you keep them? _____

Do you presently have any close friends? _____ How many? _____

How many hours a day do you spend on the Internet, texting? _____

Please list your 3 greatest strengths:

1. _____

2. _____

3. _____

Please list your 3 greatest weaknesses:

1. _____

2. _____

3. _____

Please indicate how often the following thoughts occur to you:

	Never	Rarely	Sometimes	Frequently
Life is hopeless				
No one cares about me				
I am bad				
I am a failure				
I am deficient				
Most people don't like me				
I am so depressed				
I want to die				
I want to hurt someone				
Something is wrong with me				
God is disappointed in me				
I can't be forgiven				
I should be punished				
I can't concentrate				
I can't do anything right				
I don't belong anywhere				
Why am I so different?				
I have no emotions				
I am going crazy				
People hear my thoughts				
I hear voices in my head				
Someone is watching me				

Please indicate any of the following that are a problem for you:

☐ Anger/aggression	☐ Alcohol use	☐ Antisocial behavior
☐ Anxiety	☐ Avoiding people	☐ Can't get along
☐ Can't keep a job	☐ Can't make decisions	☐ Can't relax
☐ Can't slow down	☐ Chest pain	☐ Depression
☐ Difficulty concentrating	☐ Disorientation	☐ Disorganized thoughts
☐ Dizziness	☐ Don't like being alone	☐ Don't like free time
☐ Drug use	☐ Eating disorder	☐ Elevated mood
☐ Fatigue	☐ Fears/phobias	☐ Financial problems
☐ Hallucinations	☐ Headaches	☐ Heart palpitations
☐ Hopelessness	☐ Impulsiveness	☐ Irritability
☐ Judgment errors	☐ Loneliness	☐ Memory problems
☐ Mood shifts	☐ Nightmares	☐ No appetite
☐ No fun in life	☐ No friends	☐ Panic attacks
☐ Recurring thoughts	☐ Sexual difficulties	☐ Shyness
☐ Sick often	☐ Sleep problems	☐ Speech problems
☐ Suicidal thoughts	☐ Suicidal plans	☐ Trembling
☐ Withdrawing	☐ Worrying	☐ Isolation

Childhood History

Mother's health during her pregnancy with you and during your infancy:

_____

Check any of the following that applied to you during childhood:

☐ Night-terrors   ☐ Bed-wetting   ☐ Sleepwalking   ☐ Thumb-sucking
☐ Stammering   ☐ Fears   ☐ Happy childhood ☐ Unhappy childhood

Health during childhood? _____

List childhood illnesses:

_____

_____

Any surgeries? At what age(s)? _____

_____

_____

Childhood games and interests: _____

_____

Interests during adolescence: _____

_____

Age beginning school? _____ Age finishing school? _____

Scholastic achievements/disabilities: _____

_____

Athletic achievements/disabilities/injuries: _____

_____

Were you bullied or given a nickname? _____ If so, what? _____

Grade/degree reached? _____ Age _____

Family History

Mother's health during her pregnancy with you and during your infancy:

_____

Mother's present age? _____ If deceased, how old was she when she died? _____

Father's present age? _____ If deceased, how old was he when he died? _____

How did your parents behave toward each other: _____

_____

Briefly describe the atmosphere in the family: _____

_____

If your parents separated or divorced, how old were you? _____

Were you adopted or raised by someone other than your biological parents? _____

If so, who? Between what ages? _____

Please list your brothers and sisters (in birth order):

Name	Brother/Sister	Years Older/Younger	Occupation	Marital Status

Briefly describe your relationships with your brothers and sisters:

Childhood: _____

Current: _____

Your Mother (or mother substitute)

Brief description:

_____

_____

Describe any problems (alcoholism, depression, disability, etc.) she may have had that may have affected your childhood development:

_____

_____

How much time did she spend with you when you were a child?   _____

How did she discipline/punish you?

_____

_____

How did she reward you?

_____

_____

Briefly describe your relationship with her then:

_____

_____

Briefly describe your relationship with her now:

_____

_____

Your Father (or father substitute)

Brief description:

_____

_____

Describe any problems (alcoholism, depression, disability, etc.) he may have had that may have affected your childhood development:

_____

How much time did he spend with you when you were a child?   _____

_____

How did he discipline/punish you?

_____

_____

How did he reward you?

_____

_____

Briefly describe your relationship with him then:

_____

_____

Briefly describe your relationship with him now:

_____

_____

Sexual and Relationship History

Parental attitudes toward sex?   _____

How and when did you first learn about sex? _____

When and how did you first become aware of your sexual feelings?

_____

_____

How have you felt about your own sexuality?

_____

_____

At what age did you begin dating? _____ Having sex? _____

Have you ever been raped? _____ Sexually molested? _____

Are you married/long-term partner? _____ Divorced? _____ # of times? _____

Please describe your sexual orientation/identity:

_____

_____

Briefly describe your dating/relationship history:

_____

_____

Have you noticed any patterns in your relationships? Please describe:

_____

_____

Children; please list each child's name and age:

Name	Age	Name	Age	Name	Age

Experienced Miscarriages (dates): _____

Abortions (dates): _____

Work History

Age you started working: _____

Jobs held (in chronological order):

1. _____

2. _____

3. _____

Does your present work satisfy you? (If not, in what ways are you dissatisfied?)

_____

_____

Present salary/income: _____

Ambitions, career, or retirement plans:

_____

_____

Spirituality

Briefly describe your present spiritual/religious life:

_____

_____

How important is it, relative to the rest of your life?

_____

_____

Please list any other information or topics that you believe are important for me to understand:

_____

_____

Group History

Please list your experience(s) as a group member and approximate date in each group:

_____

_____

_____

Adapted with permission from Daniel Taube, Ph.D., (personal correspondence, 2009) who acknowledges that this work is a compilation of prior versions created by numerous authors.

Chapter 7: Group Guidelines/Group Agreements

What follows is a copy of the Group Office Policy that I have all new group members sign during our initial screening session.

Sample Private Practice Group Office Policy

YOUR LETTERHEAD HERE

Office Policies

Confidentiality

Therapy involves talking about very private, sensitive topics with the group therapist and the group. To some extent, the group leader's ability to help you will depend on how open you can be about yourself, your ideas, feelings and actions. Psychotherapy is not like a medical doctor visit. Instead, it calls for a very active effort on your part. During our sessions and at home, you will have to work on issues we talk about for the therapy to be most successful.

Psychotherapy can have benefits and risks. Since therapy often involves discussing unpleasant aspects of your life, you may experience uncomfortable feelings like sadness, guilt, anger, frustration, loneliness, and helplessness. On the other hand, therapy often leads to better relationships, solutions to specific problems, and significant reductions in feelings of distress. But there are no guarantees about what you will experience.

The law has made it your therapist's duty to keep information about you confidential so that you can feel free to talk openly and so that your right to privacy is protected. This means that, generally, your therapist may not discuss your case with anyone or send out information about you without your written permission.

I also want you to know that I must keep records of your therapy including: this consent form; notes of our sessions (these may cover your problems and goals, dates we met, topics we covered, and any special issues that arise); brief notes of phone contacts; and a summary at the end of treatment. These records are just as confidential as what we talk about during sessions.

Exceptions to Confidentiality

There are some legal exceptions to confidentiality. Although these situations are rare or may not happen at all, it is important for you to understand the limits of confidentiality.

1. If you threaten to harm someone else, and I believe this threat is serious, I am required under the law to take steps to protect people who may be in danger. These steps include calling the person or people who are threatened and notifying the police.

2.   If you threaten to cause severe harm to yourself, and I believe the threat is serious, I am ethically required to try as best I can to protect you. This might include talking to you about voluntarily going to a hospital, or having you placed in a hospital even without your permission, or calling a mental health crisis team or the police.

3.   If I suspect that any child, elderly person, or dependent adult is or has been abused or neglected, the law requires that I report this to the appropriate county agency. These laws are meant to protect children, elders, and dependent adults from being hurt.

4.   If you are or may become involved in any kind of lawsuit or administrative procedure (such as a worker's compensation claim), and you or your attorney would like to tell the court about your mental or emotional health, you may not be able to keep your records or your therapy private in court. Also, if you bring a legal action against your psychotherapist, you will not be able to keep your records or your therapy private in court. Please consult your attorney about these matters.

5.   If I receive a subpoena or a court order asking for your records, I may be required to give the court the specific information that it wants. If your records are requested of me under the auspices of the Patriot Act, the (current) law prohibits me from informing you that this has occurred. If this is of concern, please be sure to discuss it with me in person.

6.   If you use insurance, you will almost always have to sign a consent form for me to disclose certain information to the insurance company. Many insurance companies require that I provide a diagnosis, develop and send treatment plans, progress reports, and other records. Please be aware that once information is sent to the insurance company, I no longer have any control over who sees it. Almost all insurance companies state that they will keep the information confidential, but I have no way to assure that. Some insurance companies share the information they receive with a national medical information data bank. Before any information is sent, I will talk with you about what I have written. You do have a choice about whether to release this information to an insurance company, but if you do not, most insurance programs will not pay for services.

7.   If you are seeing me as a group member, I ask that each person involved in the therapy group promise not to reveal the names of fellow group members or discuss in ways that could identify fellow members, issues that are discussed in therapy with anybody who is not part of treatment. However, I cannot guarantee that members of group will keep this promise.

8.   In the event that I am out of town or am unavailable I have an agreement with colleagues that they will take emergency calls in my absence. I have chosen these licensed mental health care providers with great care and will only share information with them that will allow them to provide appropriate care for you. This may include a summary of your diagnosis, any specific areas of concern, our treatment plan, and how to contact you if I am unable to do so myself.

Release of Information

If you ever want me to share information with someone else (for example, your individual psychotherapist, psychiatrist, physician, or an insurance company), I will ask you to sign a consent form allowing me to exchange information with the person you want me to talk to or send records to. We will talk about this before you sign the consent.

Fee Information

Fee Schedule

My basic fee for each 50-minute session screening/preparation session is $____.00. The fee for group is $___.00 per 90 minute session, payable at the beginning of the month. I have a limited number of hours set aside for working with people who cannot afford my full fee. If you cannot afford my full fee and I have the time open, we can negotiate a fee that is affordable for you.

Occasionally, my fees might increase due to inflation and cost of living increases. If I decide it is necessary to change my fee, I will talk with the group about it beforehand.

Payment and Insurance

Payment must be made at the time services are rendered or once you start group, at the start of the month. It is my policy to have patients pay me directly with a check. Although I am no longer on any insurance panels, I can provide you with a bill that you can submit to your insurance company for reimbursement.

Missed Appointments

Group members are expected to give the group as much advance notice of anticipated absences and vacations as possible. Each member will have the group fee waived for 2 sessions a year for vacation time. If you are unable to come to group, please notify me immediately. Since your place in group cannot be filled by anyone else, you will be charged for missed sessions unless it is a medical or unavoidable emergency. If you need to miss a session due to an emergency or illness, and give me and the group as much notice as possible, I will not charge you. If you have difficulty keeping your commitment to attend group weekly we will need to discuss this in group. If you have a chronic medical problem that may result in your needing to cancel appointments, we can discuss an alternative arrangement.

I have read and understood the above information and received a copy of this form.

Signature: _____

Date: _____

NOTE: Health Insurance Portability and Accountability Act (HIPAA)

Clinicians wishing to meet HIPAA guidelines should include a statement in their HIPAA notifications clearly informing patients that one of the limitations to confidentiality occurs when the therapist becomes unavailable due to an unforeseeable accident, emergency, or medical issue. The statement should include the fact that if this type of absence occurs, the therapist has an agreement with another licensed professional to contact the patients and become custodian of the records if necessary. Since HIPAA is designed to address privacy policies and practices, clinicians who are following HIPAA guidelines should include this information in their written office policies and/or informed consent forms.

Disclaimers: Your state or guild may require that additional language and disclaimers be included in the text of your office policy.

The information in these forms does not represent legal advice and should not be relied upon as such. As with all legal matters, check with an attorney practicing in your state to ensure that the material in these documents do not run contrary to your state's laws.

As mentioned earlier, I have new group members review, discuss, and sign my termination agreement during our final preparation session. What follows is a copy of the form that I created.

Sample Termination Agreement

YOUR LETTERHEAD HERE

Talking About Termination: Rare Opportunities

Most people have never experienced a clear, honest termination with significant people in their lives. Therapy groups offer an opportunity for this kind of termination which is often the most challenging and rewarding phase of treatment. These guidelines are designed to maximize a positive experience for both the member who is leaving and the group.

The Major Stages of a Healthy Termination

1. Open discussion when thinking of leaving the group and allowing group input into the decision. Hopefully, this will take place before you have decided to leave.

2. Open discussion of the pros and cons, for you, of leaving group at this time. This entails reviewing your initial goals, progress made, and addressing how you want your departure to be different from past terminations in your life. At the conclusion of this stage, it is important to set a target date for your departure.

3. Focusing on your actual termination issues.

When You Want to Leave Group

To make the most of the termination phase, group members agree to let the group know when they **begin** to think about leaving group. This lets the other group members know if you are finding it difficult to continue, feel your needs are not being met, as well as, when you feel you have accomplished yours goals.

Stage One

Sharing with the Group Your Thoughts and Reasons for Wanting to Leave

The goal is to discuss, as NON-DEFENSIVELY and OPENLY as possible, the wide range of reasons that have contributed to your wanting to end your participation in group. Remember that being in group may be one of the most challenging, possibly painful, yet rich, experiences you have ever dealt with. Allow input from the group regarding their feelings and thoughts about your wish to leave. Members need to be free to share THEIR personal, emotional reactions as separate from their thoughts about what is in your best interest. A challenge for the departing group member is to listen, as openly as possible, to others' comments, and to consider and weigh their input before making a final decision. Another challenge is to remember that the decision is yours to make, no one can, or should try to, force you to stay if you are clear that you want to leave the group. Leave-taking involves some pain. By giving yourself and the group enough time to have closure, you will be making room for the sadness of leaving and the joy of celebrating your accomplishments.

Stage Two

After You Decide to Leave

Your termination will be more valuable if you and the group are clear about what you want to accomplish before you leave. It will help if this is discussed openly with the group. Use the group's input to decide on a length of time that will be best for you **and** the group to address your termination. It will help everyone concerned to have a specific target date. A **minimum** of 4 sessions is suggested to wrap up. The longer you have been in group, the more you and the group will benefit from a longer termination period. In **some** cases it may be best to allow one month of termination for every year in group.

Defining a Meaningful Termination Process

1. Understand and discuss, in group, your history of leaving relationships, having relationships end, and how you want this termination to be different.
2. Identify and clarify, with the group's help, any unfinished areas between yourself and other group members, including the leader. Include old, unresolved issues from prior sessions to be addressed and resolved to the best of your own and the group's abilities.

Decide how you want to feel when you leave the group. Discuss patterns that may interfere with this goal and enlist the group's help in finding ways of leaving that will increase the likelihood that you will depart with a feeling of accomplishment.

Stage Three

Stick to Saying Goodbye

The termination phase is one of the most difficult and important phases of therapy. The focus and priority of the departing group member needs to be on the actual work of termination. At the same time, the group needs to proceed with its own work. This process is facilitated by the departing member refraining from bringing up new material, issues or crises that cannot be dealt with effectively if the priority is to leave group. By spreading the termination process out over a period of time, the group can continue its work while saying goodbye at the same time. Some groups decide to allot a set amount of time per session to address the pending termination.

Reasons for Taking all this Time

Leaving prematurely denies the member and the group the opportunity to complete the therapeutic process begun together. Saying goodbye is usually painful and difficult. Group members often feel a strong pull to leave in anger, rather than take the time, over a few sessions, to allow a calm, well-reasoned series of open discussions. By setting an adequate amount of time to terminate, each group member is encouraged to deal with unfinished business and discuss openly his or her feelings about the departing member. The therapist will help resolve disagreements and encourage the group to have the departing member leave with a feeling of accomplishment.

Suggested Topics for Talking about your Termination

The following discussion topics are included here to help you when you begin to deal with termination. The goal of doing the work described below is to reduce the chances that you will discover unfinished business after you have left the group.

- Begin to list, celebrate, and acknowledge your hard work and accomplishments
- Raise and discuss issues or feelings that you and or group members wanted to express but have not
- Review your initial goals
- Discuss progress, changes, and benefits of being in group
- Begin to discuss the challenges and difficulties in relation to other group members and the leader, as well as progress made in these areas
- Discuss and agree upon a realistic timeline for termination
- Discuss ways in which the group can help in your termination process
- Discuss and decide on a ritual or termination process that will feel best to you and the group.

Anticipating Future Challenges or Areas of Difficulty and Planning to Reduce Risk of Set-Backs

- How will you replace the support and problem-solving assistance, feedback, and feeling of belonging that you get from this group?
- What resources do you have now that you did not have when you started group?
- Using the group's input, list your personal warning signs that indicate you need more support
- List the people who will be there for you and people you can call
- What kinds of self-care techniques can you remind yourself to do?

Signature: _____   Date Signed: _____

Copy Received: ☐ Yes   ☐ No

Sample Group Agreements

As discussed earlier, having written group agreements helps members understand the expectations for members of the group they are joining. You may want to review the benefits of group agreements discussed in Chapter 3, page 28.

What follows is a group agreement from an outpatient treatment center that specializes in addictions of all sorts. They use a different kind of group agreement that conveys the wide range of issues group agreements can address.

Commitment

At Impulse Treatment Center we require a three month **commitment** to be part of a group; regular attendance and punctuality are expected throughout whatever time period you attend.

At ITC we view the word **commitment** as an action, not just a feeling. **Commitment** requires showing up unless you are ill, have a scheduled vacation, or an emergency. A **minimum of** 75% **attendance** is required in order to continue; three absences in a row may require meeting with your group leader. Following are some other examples of what **commitment** is and what it is not:

Commitment Is Not.....	Commitment Is.....
Saying you're committed to the group but having a list of urgent reasons why you need to be elsewhere.	Showing up. Keeping track of emergencies or scheduled vacations and talking about the impact on you and the group. Recognizing when you can no longer keep your commitment to the group.
Not showing up for group due to an emergency and expecting everyone to be fine.	Calling and letting the group leader know as soon as you can what the emergency is and that you are safe.
Justifying irregular attendance with the belief that you have no impact on the other group members. Nothing much happened in your life this week anyway.	Understanding that your presence impacts the group and the group loses something important when you are not there. Who you are has value.
Arriving late on a regular basis or leaving early.	Being on time for group and remaining to the end.
Not showing up for group because you are ashamed of yourself or your behavior, angry, sad or feeling hopeless.	Showing up for group even if you are ashamed of yourself or your behavior, angry, sad or feeling hopeless.
Showing up for group but keeping your shameful, angry, sad or hopeless feelings to yourself.	Bringing your feelings to group and practicing owning them.
Calling in an "acceptable" reason to skip group when you really want a night off.	Talking in group about what is going on that makes it so hard to show up and why self-care would include not coming to therapy.
Showing up for group and waiting to speak until someone else notices that you haven't.	Claiming your place in group even if you don't believe what you have to share is important.
Cancelling group because you have to take your mom, your friend, your neighbor's son to an appointment.	Telling your mom, your friend, your neighbor that you would be happy to help them out but they'll need to schedule their appointment for a different time/day because you have something important you have to do for yourself.

Reprinted with permission of the Impulse Treatment Center, Don Mathews MFT, Director. Author: Joan Gold, MFT; personal correspondence, December 27, 2013.

For Self-Help Groups

Self-help organizations that provide peer-led support groups come in many forms. Some are led by professional, licensed leaders and others by patients, family members, or volunteers. They rarely provide either screening or follow-up. To protect and to clarify member's expectations, I have helped numerous organizations create group agreements that fit their population. The following sample contains language that can clarify expectations and assist non-profit, self-help organizations make their group offerings safer. Feel free to use part or all of this sample.

Sample Self-Help Support Group Agreements/Guidelines Templates

Name/Logo of Organization: _____

The _____ Foundation support groups offer an opportunity to gather to share feelings and information that are unique to those living with _____. Please read through the guidelines below so that you understand what you can expect from our support groups and what we expect from our group participants.

It is important to understand the limitations of a support group. _____'s support groups are designed to provide support, camaraderie, information sharing, and a chance to meet others in like situations. A wide range of thoughts and feelings may be expressed in an atmosphere of acceptance. It is an opportunity to make connections with other people who are living with _____. These connections may continue outside of the group and sustain attendees during the ups and downs with _____. We do NOT offer individual or group therapy and this is NOT an opportunity for counseling, diagnosis, or treatment of disorders. Our focus is on encouraging and supporting one another. The _____ support groups are not a replacement for professional medical or mental health help.

Remember: Confidentiality is important to all attendees. Confidentiality allows people to feel safe in expressing personal issues. Sharing something personal can be the first step toward acknowledgement, acceptance, and finding healthy ways to live with your limitations. To ensure confidentiality for all participants, you are asked not to reveal any participant's name or personal issues outside of the group. If you feel the need to discuss a group's dynamic or something that you experienced because of someone else's story, make use of an "I statement" (for example, "One parent was extremely angry with her child for not cooperating with treatments. I felt……, I cried…….. I resented….. I wanted to…. I remembered…..etc."). Be aware that most facilitators are licensed and practicing professional counselors. They are required by law to report incidences of child, elder, or spousal abuse.

Tips for Getting More Out of Your Group Experience

Plan to arrive on time and stay for the entire group session unless your medical condition makes it unwise to do so. This will allow the group to build trust, establish a focus and continuity that will be helpful. If you must leave your group early or enter after the group has begun, do so as inconspicuously as possible. Due to the vulnerability of those who participate, avoid making assumptions about another's situation or expressing harsh judgments. If you disagree with another member, use "I" statements ("I like to handle that differently" or "I feel uncomfortable with what you're saying," etc.).

Only one person should speak at a time. Respect your support group members, their situations, emotions, and perspectives. Do not interrupt, do not talk over others, do not laugh at or make fun of other members of the group. Limit suggestions to others unless they are asking for ideas and advice. Understand that it is not your job to fix someone else's feelings or make them feel better. Also, remember these guidelines.

- ❖ No one person is allowed to take over the group. Beware of talking too much, controlling the topic, or expecting too much from the group. Give quieter members an opportunity to share.
- ❖ It is okay to sit and listen and remain totally silent. Simply say, "pass," when people are sharing in the group and it is your turn.
- ❖ In many groups, attendees like to share and exchange medical information. Understand that the final word about any medical treatment or medicine should come from you with input from your physicians.
- ❖ Avoid doctor bashing. If you want to discuss an uncomfortable experience with the medical system, leave out names.
- ❖ If a facilitator has been assigned to your group, that person's role is to serve as a guide for the group. The facilitator is a resource for your group. If you are unhappy with how the group is going, speak up and allow the facilitator to intervene.
- ❖ It is important to put your feelings into words, not actions. If a group member becomes verbally or physically abusive toward another member, that person will be asked to leave immediately.

I have read and understand these guidelines. I agree to follow them. I understand that _____'s support groups are for support, discussion and encouragement only. They do not provide professional therapy.

Print Name: _____   Signature _____

This next sample is a group agreement written by a Community Circle. It incorporates many of the core ingredients for a safe peer-led support group.

"As members of a Community Circle (TIE) Group of the Mt. Diablo Unitarian Universalist Church, we gather together to intentionally share in our search for community, for significant connection with each other, for a personal sense of deeper meaning in our lives, and for spirituality.

To remain healthy and profound, groups depend on the kindness and openness of everyone involved. Our small groups are founded on a covenant, a sacred promise of meaningful relationship, made by all the participants with each other. The practicing of the covenant can be a fulfilling way to deepen one's experience while strengthening the respect and caring that these groups offer.

Our Covenant with Each Other

- We commit to guarding the confidentiality of what is shared here.
- Sharing is voluntary.
- We will have an equal opportunity to be heard without interruption.
- We are encouraged to speak from our own personal experience and life, sharing feelings and beliefs rather than judgments, opinions or disagreements.
- We will respect each other by listening with acceptance, compassion and openness.
- We agree to be punctual and to inform the facilitator(s) if we will be absent.
- We commit to attending every session, recognizing that sometimes life intervenes and forces us to miss.
- We commit to listen with our hearts as well as with our ears."

Reprinted with permission of the Mount Diablo Unitarian Universalist Church, Rev. Leslie Takahashi Morris; personal correspondence, November 3, 2013.

The following group agreement/guidelines for a monthly interest/networking/support group whose purpose is creative brainstorming, gives the flavor of the meetings, and how the leader keeps the group on task and productive:

- "Don't tell stories when you're making a suggestion
- Give only one brief action idea per turn
- No questions during brainstorming
- Honor this safe space; don't criticize ideas - including your own
- Outrageously impudent suggestions are encouraged
- Piggyback on previous ideas
- Offer alternatives to ideas you think are not appropriate
- If you think of an idea after the brainstorming is over, email your idea to the person who asked the question

- Respect the speaker; don't interrupt
- In this room, in this circle, there are NO WRONG ANSWERS
- There are no expectations concerning what you do with your list.
- PLEASE don't tell stories when you're making a suggestion!!
- If it's your question that's being brainstormed, just take it all in.
- Hear the information as new -even if it isn't.
- (NOTE: Add your own guidelines if you like.)"

Reprinted with permission: personal correspondence, Anita Gold, Founder/Moderator, November 20, 2014.

Chapter 8: Sample Online Group Agreements

Netiquette: Keeping Online Groups Safe

There are almost as many types of structures, policies, group agreements and designs as there are online groups, interactive blogs, etc. As with all groups, the leader(s) of online groups need to decide who they want as members, define the group's objectives and goals, and who they will allow to participate. As mentioned earlier, there are certain standards of what has come to be called basic Netiquette (http://www.albion.com/netiquette/). This is considered the source for basic Netiquette standards. The site provides more detailed information. Some groups choose to be moderated, while others are more laissez-faire. Online group agreements are at least as important as other group agreements.

This chapter includes samples of List Serve Agreements. They are included to provide an idea of the wide range of issues that can come up in Internet communications among group members, and what some organizations have found helpful. If you decide to read them all, notice what each group has done to increase the emotional safety and cohesion of their groups.

Sample Online Group Agreements

SAMPLE 1: COLLEGE COUNSELING ONLINE DISCUSSION GROUP

This popular online group of mental health providers sees itself as relatively unstructured regarding membership requirements. In general, they limit membership to mental health clinicians who are practicing in a specific area of their field. This first sample template is from a group of licensed mental health professionals and their trainees who work in university and college counseling centers

As with other groups, they make some exceptions and include some members who enjoy learning from different points of view. Some groups would consider these members to be in an affiliate or allied category.

They rely on the basic Netiquette standards. The leaders of this group vet each request to join the group individually, sometimes corresponding with an individual who is unknown to the group, or does not obviously meet the group's criteria. What follows is a template form of their online group agreement:

About _____ Group

[Name of Your Group]

Introductory Description is a list server based discussion group for _____interested in _____. This group was founded by [Name] _____, title_____, [Ph #] _____ [email address] _____ and [Name] _____. [Title] _____, [Ph #] _____, [email address] _____, and is administered through the _____. Please contact _____ who serves as moderator and list administrator if you have technical problems and/or questions regarding your subscription.

History of the Group

_____ group is the result of discussions among _____, who have the shared goal of hosting an ongoing and useful discussion of all topics relating to the _____ subscription to _____ [Name of your Group] is available by writing to _____ at the email above or by logging on to the list server's dedicated webpage at _____ where you can self-subscribe. We are requesting that self-subscription be limited to _____. This website allows access to the list's archives, subscription and un-subscription, as well as other list options. Our purpose in developing this list was to provide a congenial and supportive dialog about_____. In service of this we would like to encourage participants to be both frank and considerate in their dealings with others as well as being supportive of a wide range of professional experiences and perspectives in the course of carrying out this work. We would like to encourage you to refer to the Netiquette Home Page for any questions or concerns about list server etiquette or communication concerns which can be found at http://www.albion.com/netiquette/. Thank you for your interest in the _____. We look forward to hearing from you soon. Please feel free to pass this introductory message on to other _____who might be interested in this work. Best, [Founders] _____.

To see the collection of prior postings to the list, visit the _____Archives (*the current archive is only available to the list members*).

Using [_____]

To post a message to all the list members, send email to _____

You can subscribe to the list, or change your existing subscription, in the sections below.

Subscribing to [_____]

Subscribe to _____ by filling out the following form. You will be sent email requesting confirmation, to prevent others from gratuitously subscribing you. This is a private list, which means that the list of members is not available to non-members.

Your email address:	
Your name (optional):	
You may enter a privacy password below. This provides only mild security, but should prevent others from messing with your subscription. Do not use a valuable password as it will occasionally be emailed back to you in cleartext.	
If you choose not to enter a password, one will be automatically generated for you, and it will be sent to you once you've confirmed your subscription. You can always request a mail-back of your password when you edit your personal options. Once a month, your password will be emailed to you as a reminder.	
Pick a password:	
Reenter password to confirm:	
Which language do you prefer to display your messages?	English
Would you like to receive list mail batched in a daily digest?	No Yes

[_____] Subscribers

(The subscribers list is only available to the list members.)

Enter your address and password to visit the subscribers list:

Address: Password:

To unsubscribe from _____, get a password reminder, or change your subscription options enter your subscription email address:

If you leave the field blank, you will be prompted for your email address

_____ list run by _____

_____ [requires authorization]

Overview of all lists: _____

Adapted with permission; personal correspondence Joshua M. Gross, Ph.D., ABPP, CGP, FAGPA, and Anne M. Slocum McEneaney, Ph.D., ABPP, CGP, FAGPA, who acknowledge the support and generosity of Florida State University, August 12, 2014.

SAMPLE 2: THE AMERICAN GROUP PSYCHOTHERAPY ASSOCIATION LISTSERVE

The following is an example of the level of attention that increases safety for national listserve members and the organization. As you read the guidelines they created, think about which topics and challenges they face as a large multidisciplinary organization and note those sections that could be helpful for your group or organization. The American Group Psychotherapy Association (AGPA) has created what they describe as *My Communities Listserv Etiquette and Rules* (AGPA, 2013).

"AGPA's My Communities listserve provide an open forum for AGPA members to dialogue with other members who participate in their respective work or interest groups. All AGPA members are welcome to participate.

My Communities listservs are a great medium with which to solicit the advice of your peers, benefit from their experience, and participate in an ongoing conversation. We hope AGPA's listserve will provide a useful and informative means of communicating with your fellow AGPA members!

Lively and candid exchanges are encouraged; however as with any community, there are also rules governing the forum. For instance, violating antitrust laws, libeling others, selling, and marketing are not permissible. Please take a moment to acquaint yourself with these important rules and etiquette. If you have questions, contact AGPA directly."

Listserv Rules and Etiquette

- Don't challenge or attack others. The discussions on the lists are meant to stimulate conversation, not create contention. Let others have their say, just as you may.
- Be courteous.
    - Email is not confidential. Any clinical information should be thoroughly cleansed of identifying information before being posted. Please do not transmit any content that you do not have a right to transmit.
    - Sharing or exchanging information about fees charged in a member's practice may be an antitrust law violation, as price-fixing, and therefore is prohibited.
    - All defamatory, abusive, profane, threatening, offensive, or illegal materials are prohibited. Do not transmit any content that is defamatory, vulgar, or illegal. Discussion as to whether a particular individual should be expelled from AGPA membership is also prohibited.
    - Remember that AGPA and other email list participants have the right to reproduce postings to My Communities.
    - Include a signature tag on all messages. Include your name, affiliation, location, and email address.
    - State concisely and clearly the specific topic of the comments in the subject line. This allows members to respond more appropriately to your posting and makes it easier for members to search the archives by subject.
    - Do not post commercial messages. This includes workshops, books, offices for rent, tapes, new groups, and supervision offered. Any use of the listserv for

commercial purposes threatens the organization's non-profit tax status. Contact people directly with products and services that you believe would help them.

- Send your message only to the most appropriate list(s). Only send a message to the entire list when it contains information that everyone can benefit from.

- Send messages such as "thanks for the information" or "me, too" to individuals - not to the entire list. Do this by scrolling down to the links at the bottom of the message where you can reply to the individual directly.

- Do not send administrative messages, such as "remove me from the list" or "login problems," through the listserv. If you prefer not to receive any emails from the listserv, you can unsubscribe directly from the listserv email message you received. In order to do so, scroll to the bottom of the email message until you see the "Manage your Community settings" menu. Click on the link under the UNSUBSCRIBE item and you will be directed to a web page where you can select which listservs you want to unsubscribe from. If you're having any trouble navigating this section, please contact [INSERT NAME] for help. Please note that unsubscribing from the listserv does not remove you from the community and you can still enjoy online access to all discussions at your convenience. You can also subscribe to the listserv again any time in the future.

- Do not use personal data about other users of My Communities.

- The default setting for all listserv emails is Digest. With this setting, you will receive a daily compilation of all messages in the community in one email message once per day. Do not respond to digest email messages using reply as there is no subject line and the entire digest attaches to your email. If you would like to participate in discussions, we recommend cutting and pasting the message into a new email to accompany your reply, going online to the community to reply or choosing the Individual setting for message delivery."

Disclaimer and Legal Rules

My Communities is provided as a service of the American Group Psychotherapy Association. AGPA accepts no responsibility for the opinions and information posted on this site by others.

Under no circumstances will AGPA be liable in any way for any content, including, but not limited to, for any errors or omissions in any content, or for any loss or damage of any kind incurred as a result of the use of any content transmitted via the My Communities.

AGPA does not actively monitor the site for inappropriate postings and does not on its own undertake editorial control of postings. However, in the event that any inappropriate posting is brought to AGPA's attention, AGPA will take all appropriate action. AGPA reserves the right to terminate access to any user who does not abide by these guidelines."

Adapted/Reprinted with permission from the American Group Psychotherapy Association; email correspondence, October 14, 2014.

SAMPLE 3: AMERICAN PSYCHOLOGICAL ASSOCIATION'S COMMUNITIES

The American Psychological Association, which serves 130,000 members, has created these guidelines for its members-only forum:

'Welcome to APA Communities. APA Communities is a closed social network meaning that it is accessible by APA members and affiliates and APA division members only. This new community platform will allow you to connect with and share information and ideas with your psychology colleagues from anywhere you access the internet.

If you have any difficulties logging in, please contact via telephone at _____ from hours_____ OR email address _____.

"If you subscribed to this forum and especially if you send messages to the forum, you are agreeing to these rules. The rules are:

Rule 1: Do not use the forum for illegal purposes, including but not limited to defamation, violation of intellectual property laws, violation of antitrust or unfair competition laws or violation of criminal laws.

Rule 2: Do not intentionally interfere with or disrupt other forum members, network services, or network equipment. This includes distribution of unsolicited advertisement or chain letters, propagation of computer worms and viruses, and use of the network to make unauthorized entry to any other machine accessible via the Forum.

Rule 3: Do not use the Forum for commercial purposes. "Commercial" as used for purposes of evaluating listserv messages means communications whose primary purpose is to advance the business or financial interests of any person or entity, or otherwise to promote a financial transaction for the benefit of the author directly or indirectly. Examples of prohibited communications include advertisements for products or services, notices regarding rental of office space, or direct solicitations of listserv members to purchase products or services.

[Examples of messages that may be of financial benefit to listserv members but are not prohibited because they do not inure to the financial benefit of the author include news of job listings or position openings, or discussion of professionally-related products or services where the listserv member conveying the information is not in the business of selling the products or services. Announcements that provide useful professional information to List members but may also have some incidental commercial benefit to the sender (e.g., an author who is a listmember merely advising the List of publication of a professional book) typically would not be "commercial" for purposes of this restriction.]

Rule 4: Do not use this forum for any communication that could be construed in any way as support for or opposition to any candidate for a federal, state or local public office. The Federal law providing for the _____ tax exempt status absolutely forbids the use of APA _____.

Important Email Addresses to Remember:

Email Address is the address you use to send messages to your list. This is how you would communicate with other members of your list. Your list address is: _____

NOTE: The ability to send messages to your list depends on the type of list you have (forums, newsletter, etc.). Refer to the accompanying Welcome Message for more information or contact the List Owner of this list.

The List Owner email address is the address of the owner of the list. This is the person you should contact if you have any trouble with the list, or have any questions. The address of your List Owner is: _____

Listserv Web Interface:

The Listserv Web Interface is a website where you can handle all Listserv business. The Web Interface is located at _____ recommends using the Web Interface due to its ease of use. The Web Interface allows you to do the following through your web browser:

- Post Messages
- Read Messages
- Search/Review Archives of ALL messages posted to the list
- Change personal user settings
- Download Attachments
- Manage personal user settings for multiple lists at the same time
- Join or leave this and other lists

Informational Resources:

The _____ strives to make your Listserv experience enjoyable. Therefore the _____ provides Help Guides and FAQ's to help you use Listserv.

Web Interface Help Guide – This Guide is a Tutorial on how to use Listserv's Web Interface. Please review this guide before using the Web Interface.

Things to remember:

Auto-Reply messages – Auto-reply messages such as "Out of Office" Messages can cause complications depending on the way [Name of group or organization] _____ is configured. A mail loop could be caused, sending out several messages to Listserv, your fellow List Subscribers, and also back to you. You should either temporarily disable your Name of group or organization] _____ account or set up a rule in your email client to ignore messages from _____ email address of group or organization. For information on "Out of Office Messages," visit your Name of group or organization] email contact] _____.

Adapted/Reprinted with permission from the American Psychological Association; email correspondence, October 30, 2014.

SAMPLE 4: AMERICAN PSYCHOLOGICAL ASSOCIATION FORUM'S SOCIAL MEDIA POLICIES

This next sample is based upon the social media policies created by the American Psychological Association for it's members:

"This is an Official _____ [Name of Organization] _____ Forum, and as such, subject to the rules set forth here. This Forum is administered and monitored by [Name of Organization] _____. Any person or content that violates any of _____ [Name of Organization] social media policies may be removed from the site, at the sole discretion of _____ [Name of Organization].

By unanimous action of the _____ [Name of Organization], the following communications policy is in effect as of (insert date): _____.

First and foremost, public social networks are not private. Some may be open only to invited or approved members; but even then, users should not expect privacy among the members. If you choose to participate on such Forums, assume that anything you post will be seen, read, and open for comment. Anything you say, post, link to, comment on, upload, etc., can and may be used against you by your peers, colleagues, employer, potential employers, fellow members, and so on.

_____ [Name of Organization's] social and professional communication tools (listservs, Facebook page, etc.) are used by the entire cross-section of _____ [Name of Organization] members: clinicians, researchers, academics, senior professionals, students, and non-psychologists; in the U.S., Canada, and abroad. Different perspectives are expected and welcomed. Any participant may post a message and all will see it.

Messages may be program announcements, job postings, information of professional interest, etc. Members may post questions, seek advice or debate professional issues. By embracing the following standards, we all contribute to a climate of trust and collegiality that encourages friendly, informed, and spontaneous discourse.

Professional debates can create strong differences of opinion, which may be expressed in a constructive manner; but personal attacks and offensive comments are inappropriate, not in the spirit of _____ [Name of Organization], and against the policy of all associated communications tools. Inappropriate behaviors include, but are not limited to, name-calling and other ad hominem comments. Use of profanity is explicitly disallowed.

Please observe all copyright laws as they pertain to the Internet. The forwarding of any individual's postings or emails to you or others without her or his permission constitutes a "back-channel communication." To do so is a violation of our communications policies. If you wish to forward communications originating from another individual, you must document the expressed granting of permission to forward the originator's comments. To do this, you must include with your forwarded message(s) the originator's permission to forward the message(s) in question to the listserv.

Be considerate of the length of your message; extended documents, or even a long series of abstracts, may be more information than all readers are interested in receiving. Alternatively, you may direct interested parties to contact you off-list, or provide a link to another more comprehensive site.

[NOTE: Include if your organization has non-profit status, and consider including even if your organization does not.] Federal law providing for the _____ [Name of Organization] tax exempt status absolutely forbids the use of _____ [Name of Organization] resources or facilities, including _____ [Name of Organization] communications tools, in any way that would even appear to support or oppose a political candidate for local, state or national public office.

_____ (Name of Organization, including committee responsible for such decisions] may or may not choose to endorse a candidate for _____ [Name of Organization] President. If so, a statement to that effect may appear through _____ [Name of Organization] media. Individual participants may choose to use _____ [Name of Organization] communications tools to provide their perspectives on _____ [Name of Organization] Presidential candidates in a positive, collegial manner. All eligible _____ [Name of Organization] members are urged to vote in the _____ [Name of Organization] Presidential elections.

Listservs may be utilized by students to invite participation in surveys. Students are cautioned, however, that not all results obtained via the use of listserv surveys may be deemed representative, generalizable, or defensible. Students should consult their institution's IRB committee for additional cautions.

The list administrator will refer any posting deemed to be in potential violation of communications policy to the _____ [Name of Organization] for review. [Author's Note: having a system that includes more than one individual in place to conduct this kind of review is extremely important.] A subcommittee will determine when activity is in violation of policy. If a subscriber violates policy, he or she will be given email notification of the violation, and be advised that if a second violation occurs, the subscriber may be blocked from participation in _____ [Name of Organization] communications system(s) at the discretion of the Publications subcommittee [Or title of committee your organization has in place]. A third violation will automatically result in removal. The minimum length of suspension for violating policy is six months from the date of notification of removal.

Any subscriber who has been removed from _____ [Name of Organization] communications system(s) can make a request in writing to the full Board of _____ [Name of Organization] for consideration to be reinstated. The request for reinstatement must include an acknowledgement of the violation(s) of policy that led to removal, an agreement to conform to the policies in effect, and recognition that an additional violation (of any kind) will result in permanent revocation of all _____ [Name of Organization] communications privileges. Requests for reinstatement will be considered by the Board and/or Executive Committee during their semi-annual meetings, which typically occur in January/February and August of each year. Requests must be submitted to the Board at least 30 days prior to the next semi-annual meeting via the Division administrative office _____ [Organization's Email Contact Address].

The resources (hardware, software, and technical assistance) for this effort are provided without charge by the _____ [Name of Organization] as a public service. If you subscribed, and especially if you send messages, you are agreeing to four rules: (1) The media may not be used for illegal purposes (such as defamation, violation of intellectual property law, violation of antitrust or criminal law). (2) Participants may not intentionally interfere with or disrupt other forum members, network services, or network equipment. (3) The media may not be used for commercial purposes. (4) The media may not be used for any communication that could be construed in any way as support for or opposition to any candidate for a federal, state or local public office. If you break these rules, you will be unsubscribed from the listserv by _____ [Name of Organization]."

Adapted/Reprinted with permission from the American Psychological Association; email correspondence, October 30, 2014.

SAMPLE 5: LIST SERVE FOR MEMBERS OF A PROFESSIONAL ORGANIZATION

The following List Serve (E-Tree) online agreement was created by Marriage and Family Therapists in Northern California. This is a very active moderated group, offering both an individual email format and a daily digest.

List Serv (E-Tree) Terms and Conditions of Use

"The _____List Serv (herein called the E-Tree), is governed by the following terms and conditions of use. Your use of the E-Tree constitutes acceptance of these terms and conditions. The most current version of these terms and conditions will always be available here on the _____website (www _____.org). The terms and conditions may change at any time, and if they do, the updated terms and conditions will be posted on the website and also sent to the E-Tree.

General Rules

The E-Tree is an unmoderated List Serv _____ does not exert any editorial control of email sent to the E-Tree, and does not take responsibility for the content of any email sent to the E-Tree.

All defamatory, abusive, profane, threatening, offensive, or illegal materials are strictly prohibited.

Maintain a respectful tone towards your colleagues who may hold differing opinions. Do not challenge or attack others. The discussions on the lists are meant to stimulate conversation, share information and resources, not to create contention.

Message content is to be directly related to our shared interests as _____. Do not send virus warnings, jokes, petitions, political endorsements or other mass mailings to the E-Tree.

Commercial messages, including 3rd party announcements, are only welcome if they are directly related to our mission_____. Please limit announcements of upcoming events and offerings to two postings.

Only send a message to the entire E-Tree when it contains information that everyone can benefit from. Responses intended for individual users should be emailed to the intended individual. Send messages such as "thanks for the information" or "me, too" to individuals-- not to the entire list.

Include a signature tag on all messages. Include your name, affiliation, location, and e-mail address on each posting.

State concisely and clearly the specific topic of the comments in the subject line. Also include the topic of the email to which you are responding in the subject section of your posting.

Include only the relevant portions of the original message in your reply, delete any header information, and put your response before the original posting.

Warn other list subscribers of lengthy messages either in the subject line or at the beginning of the message body with a line that says 'Long Message.'"

Legal and Ethical Considerations

- [Author's Note: For medical and/or mental health related list serves, insert the purpose or goals of your group here]:

- It is our goal for members of our community to feel comfortable sharing questions, concerns and resources. Maintaining confidentiality is an essential ingredient for a safe, supportive online. Ask yourself, "If someone knew this person, could they possibly recognize him or her from these details?"

- Do not forward any email, send any information or other material protected by copyright to the E-Tree without the permission of the copyright owner. By emailing such material, you warrant and represent that you own the copyright with respect to such material or that you have received permission from the copyright owner.

- By posting to the E-Tree, you grant _____ and users of the E-Tree the non-exclusive right and license to display, copy, publish, distribute, transmit, print, and use any content of your email - including any attachments or images.

- Use caution when discussing products. Information posted on the E-Tree is not considered private, and comments are subject to libel and slander laws.

- Do not post messages if they encourage or facilitate members to arrive at any agreement that either expressly or impliedly leads to illegal activities. [Author's Note: Medical or mental health list serves should consider addressing the following issues:] price fixing, a boycott of another's business, or other conduct intended to illegally restrict free trade. Messages that encourage or facilitate an agreement about the following subjects are inappropriate: prices, discounts, or terms or conditions of sale or services; salaries; profits, profit margins, or cost data; market shares; allocation of clients or territories; or selection, rejection, or termination of clients or third party payors. References to policies and practices regarding fees are allowable as long as no actual fees are disclosed.

Agreement to Terms and Conditions of Use

- Your use of the E-Tree constitutes agreements that you have read and understand the entire E-Tree terms and conditions of use, and agree to be bound by these terms and conditions for every email you send to the E-Tree. If you have questions with regard to these terms and _____ reserves the right to suspend or terminate the ability to use the E-Tree, or suspend or terminate _____ membership for users who violate these terms and conditions. Members who have been terminated from the E-Tree and/or _____ will have their cases reviewed by _____'s board of directors within 60 days.

Disclaimer

The E-Tree is provided as a service of_____. _____ accepts no responsibility for the opinions and information posted to the E-Tree on _____'s website by others. _____ disclaims all warranties with regard to information posted on the E-Tree or _____'s website, whether posted by _____ or any third party; this disclaimer includes all implied warranties of merchantability and fitness. In no event shall _____ be liable for any special, indirect, or consequential damages or any damages whatsoever resulting from loss of use, data, or profits, arising out of or in connection with the use or performance of any information posted on the E-Tree or _____'s website.

Adapted with permission; personal correspondence, Caiti Crum, LMFT, Administrator, and Kelly Sharp, LMFT, President, East Bay CAMFT August 10, 2014.

Sample 6: Online support group for chronic medical issues:

One international online forum, http://chronicbabeclub.ning.com/ describes its goal as "Helping you live an awesome life in spite of chronic illness!" starts off with "Meet Our Moderators!"

We have four main moderators on the Forum. Contact them with questions about etiquette, membership, tech support, or anything else that's confusing. Rachel is our lead moderator; Helen does a ton and she's on U.K. time; Amy is our chief spam banner (she's great at spotting them!). And of course Editrix Jenni is also here for you.

Forum Rules - Please Read!

1. Offer solutions and suggestions anytime you can. We want to build a supportive, positive community. If you're just here to complain, there's no room for that...please take complaints somewhere else.

2. Be nice. ChronicBabes are all about finding solutions, not starting arguments. Respect different points of view - you just might learn something.

3. Please don't use profanity, and we will immediately ban anyone who says anything racist, homophobic or otherwise inflammatory. Got it?

4. If you want to post a photo or two (not 10!) of yourself or something that inspires you, great - but don't use the photo or video section to advertise your business or you'll be banned immediately.

5. Have fun! As with all things ChronicBabe-related, we want the Forum to be a place where you can enjoy yourself, get fresh ideas, meet cool people and connect in a positive way. That will happen because you make it happen, so go for it!

A few words on thoughtfulness

We are a community, which means there are many of us, all from different backgrounds and experiences. When we talk on the forum, we bring unique benefits - and biases - to the table. Please use care when responding to another member's question or statement; she (or he) may be going through a hard time, or may come from a different perspective. Try to be as factually accurate and respectful as possible, and remember that medical advice from another member should never take the place of a health care provider's advice. XO Jenni

** Disclaimer **

Babes, we are not doctors. Nor are we lawyers. In fact, we're just a bunch of women (and a few men) who are sick and want to share resources. So please be careful what you do after reading medical advice here. Always speak to your health care professional before trying a new medication, supplement, exercise routine, etc. ChronicBabe.com and its staff are not liable if bad stuff happens to you, and we would hate for bad stuff to happen to you! So be smart, savvy, and do your own research. XO Jenni, the Editrix."

Reprinted with permission of Jenni Prokopy, Forum Founder; personal correspondence, August 10, 2014.

SAMPLE 7. FATHER'S FORUM TERMS OF SERVICE AGREEMENT

This listserve agreement was created for a member's-only community serving expectant and young fathers:

"The following Terms of Service apply to your use of this Network. You are solely responsible for your conduct and your content on the Network and compliance with these terms. By registering with us or using or browsing this Network, you acknowledge that you have read, understood, and agree to be bound by these terms. This Network is not directed to anyone younger than 18 and is offered only to users 18 years of age or older. Any person who provides their personal information through this Network represents that they are 18 years of age or older.

You agree that you will not post, email or make available any content or use this Network:

In a manner that infringes, violates or misappropriates any third party's intellectual property rights or other proprietary rights or contractual rights;

In a manner that contains software viruses or any other computer code, files or programs designed to interrupt, destroy or limit the functionality of any computer software or hardware or telecommunications equipment;

To engage in spamming, "chain letters," "pyramid schemes", advertisement of illegal or controlled products or services, or other advertising or marketing activities that violate these Terms of Service, any applicable laws, regulations or generally-accepted advertising industry guidelines;

In a manner that is misleading, deceptive or fraudulent or otherwise illegal or promotes illegal activities, including engaging in phishing or otherwise obtaining financial or other personal information in a misleading manner or for fraudulent or misleading purposes;

In a manner that is libelous or defamatory, or in a way that is otherwise threatening, abusive, violent, harassing, malicious or harmful to any person or entity, or invasive of another's privacy;

In a manner that is harmful to minors in any way;

In a manner that is hateful or discriminatory based on race, color, sex, religion, nationality, ethnic or national origin, marital status, disability, sexual orientation or age or is otherwise objectionable;

To impersonate any other person, or falsely state or otherwise misrepresent your affiliation with any person or entity, or to obtain access to this Network without authorization;

To interfere or attempt to interfere with the proper working of this Network or prevent others from using this Network, or in a manner that disrupts the normal flow of dialogue with an excessive number of messages (flooding attack) to this Network, or that otherwise negatively affects other persons' ability to use this Network;

To use any manual or automated means, including agents, robots, scripts, or spiders, to access or manage any user's account or to monitor or copy this Network or the content contained therein;

To facilitate the unlawful distribution of copyrighted content;

In a manner that includes personal or identifying information about another person without that person's explicit consent;

In a manner that employs misleading email or IP addresses, or forged headers or otherwise manipulated identifiers in order to disguise the origin of content transmitted through this Network or to users; and

In a manner that constitutes or contains any form of advertising or solicitation if emailed to users who have requested not to be contacted about other services, products or commercial interests.

Additionally, you agree not to:

"Stalk" or otherwise harass anyone;

Collect, use or disclose data, including personal information, about other users without their consent or for unlawful purposes or in violation of applicable law or regulations;

Request, solicit or otherwise obtain access to usernames, passwords or other authentication credentials from any member of this Network or to proxy authentication credentials for any member of this Network for the purposes of automating logins to this Network;

Post any content containing child pornography to this Network;

Post any content that depicts or contains rape, extreme violence, murder, bestiality, incest, or other similar content;

Post any content that constitutes pornography, contains nudity, or is adult in nature.

Use automated means, including spiders, robots, crawlers, data mining tools, or the like to download data from this Network - except for Internet search engines (e.g., Google) and non-commercial public archives (e.g., archive.org) that comply with our robots.txt file, or "well-behaved" web services/RSS/Atom clients. We reserve the right to define what we mean by "well-behaved";

Post irrelevant content, repeatedly post the same or similar content or otherwise impose an unreasonable or disproportionately large load on the Network's infrastructure;

Attempt to gain unauthorized access to our computer systems or engage in any activity that disrupts, diminishes the quality of, interferes with the performance of, or impairs the functionality of, this Network;

Use this Network as a generic file hosting service;

Take any action that may undermine the feedback or ratings systems (such as displaying, importing or exporting feedback information off of this Network or for using it for purposes unrelated to this Network); and

Develop, invoke, or utilize any code to disrupt, diminish the quality of, interfere with the performance of, or impair the functionality of this Network.

To provide notice of alleged copyright infringement on this Network, please see the DMCA Notification Guidelines.

You agree not to authorize or encourage any third party to use this Network to facilitate any of the foregoing prohibited conduct. You also agree that these Network Terms of Service inure to the benefit of our service providers (including our Network platform provider) and that they may take action (including the removal of your content and disabling of your account) in order to maintain compliance with these Network Terms of Service. Technology and hosting for aspects of this Network are provided by this Network's online service provider. However, the Network Creator of this Network controls the content, membership and policy of this Network, including those pages served by such service provider on behalf of this Network. Notwithstanding anything to the contrary, by participating on this Network you agree to indemnify and hold harmless such service provider on all matters related to your interaction with others using this Network and participation with this Network."

Reprinted with permission: personal correspondence, Bruce Linton, Ph.D., Founder, Father's Forum, November 11, 2014.

Further Reading

Adapted/Reprinted with permission from the American Group Psychotherapy Association; email correspondence, October 14, 2014.

Adapted/Reprinted with permission from the American Psychological Association; email correspondence, October 30, 2014.

Adapted with permission; personal correspondence, Caiti Crum, LMFT, Administrator, and Kelly Sharp, LMFT, President, East Bay CAMFT, August 10, 2014.

Livingstone, S., Haddon, L. Gorzig, A., & Olafsson, K. (2011). Risks and safety on the internet: The perspective of European children. *Full Findings*. LSE, London: EU Kids Online: www.eukidsonline.net.

Perron, B. (2002). Online support group for caregivers of people with a mental illness. *Psychiatric Rehabilitation Journal*, 26:70-71.

Reprinted with permission; personal correspondence, Bruce Linton, Ph.D., Founder, Father's Forum, November 11, 2014.

Reprinted with permission; personal correspondence, Jenni Prokopy, Forum Founder; August 10, 2014.

Turkle, S. (2011). Alone together: Why we expect more from technology and less from each other. NY: Basic Books.

Chapter 9: Recruitment and Marketing

Group Recruitment and Marketing

- How will people find out about your group?
- Through the Internet, non-profit organizations, local hospitals, word-of-mouth?

Whether you want to recruit members for your care-partners support group or a traditional psychotherapy group, marketing is often a big obstacle.

Marketing – Who, Me?

Sound familiar? If so, you are not alone.

Only recently have graduate training programs begun to address marketing and self-promotion, traditionally considered taboo and distasteful aspects of being in private practice. When I did my pre- and post-doctoral fellowships in the '70s and for years afterwards, I didn't know anyone who admitted to advertising. Marketing was frowned upon. Practices, including mine, were built on word of mouth. Relying exclusively on word-of-mouth is no longer realistic even in large urban areas.

So, how do we overcome our disdain for marketing and do what is needed in today's fast-paced, Internet-driven world to help potential group members find us, without compromising our integrity and values? The short answer is that whether we like it or not, those of us in private practice have to be more business-minded, and think about ways to let people know about our services. Guild-based referral groups, networking groups, etc., all help.

Groups are high maintenance, especially during the initial phases and episodically throughout the life of the group. Few of us have patients calling or emailing, begging us to start a group with a ready-made compatible, well-matched group. So we are left having to promote our groups. Notice, that I said our groups, not ourselves. Yes, you need to be able to demonstrate or describe your qualifications, but you are not selling yourself or your soul if you take out an ad about your group.

Marketing may push you in areas that feel uncomfortable. Marketing requires a different skill set than comes naturally to many therapists. The sheer number of expensive marketing options can be mindboggling. From websites to online advertising, the range of possible ways to invest in recruiting group members can be overwhelming. Think strategically. Consider your priorities, time, and financial resources.

How and Where to Recruit and Market

Step One

Recruitment and Marketing: The Who, What, Where and How

1.   Think about the materials you wrote out from the tips for beginning to think about marketing, in Chapter 3, as you follow the suggestions in this section.

2.   Design an actionable, clear marketing plan.

3.   Write out and edit a 90-second elevator speech describing your group and practice it with anyone who asks you what you have been doing lately.

4.   Draft a flier that describes who will benefit from your group and what they can expect to gain. The flier should address how the group will help your target group member's pain. Remember to keep copies of your flier in the trunk of your car. You never know when someone might be interested in sharing them with a friend, co-workers, doctor, etc.

Where will You Obtain Referrals?

Think about possible referral sources and start writing them down in a list. Where can you get referrals for your group? From your individual therapy practice?

Therapists and physicians who have patients with similar issues in their practice often first think about starting a group with these patients as their core members. While many therapists do this, it is complicated and requires careful consideration. Significant controversy surrounds the issue of seeing members of one's therapy group in individual psychotherapy at the same time. Since this can cause complications in groups when not addressed skillfully, I am including a number of articles that address this important aspect of creating and maintaining groups.

I suggest that you think twice about combining patients from your current practice with patients who are not in individual therapy. Complex challenges can arise from combining your one-on-one patients with group members who don't know you other than through group participation. As in step-families, blending patients can trigger powerful reactions. Unspoken conflicts and competition are likely to arise. Patients who don't have a special relationship with the group leader may not be conscious of feeling left out unless the leader invites explicit discussion of the potential competitive, sibling and other issues. It also helps to be sensitive to group members who either cannot afford to continue seeing you while in group, and those who do not have an individual therapist other than yourself. Issues of being different, less-than, or left out can get activated and create challenges. Mixing patients this way adds an extra responsibility for the therapist to make sure that difficult emotions that get stimulated are invited and can be safely discussed. On the positive side, many therapists who see group members in both individual and group therapy feel that it allows them to see and address aspects of their patients that they would never have known about.

As with so many other challenges that arise in groups, encouraging members to talk openly about their feelings about the different relationships members have with the group leader, can detoxify secrets and open up previously unexplored family of origin issues.

The International Journal of Group Psychotherapy, Vol. 59, (1) 2009 devoted an entire special issue to combined treatment. Victor Schermer's commentary, *"On the Vicissitudes of Combining Individual and Group Psychotherapy"* is worth reading.

Six other important articles address this issue, with differing conclusions:

1.   Brabender, V. & Fallon, A. (2009). Ethical hot spots of combined individual and group therapy: Applying four ethical systems. *International Journal of Group Psychotherapy,* 59(1), 127-147.

2.   Gans, J.S. (1990). Broaching and exploring the question of combined group and individual therapy. *International Journal of Group Psychotherapy,* 40, 123-137.

3.   Kauff, P.F. (2009). Transference in combined individual and group psychotherapy. *International Journal of Group Psychotherapy,* 59, 29-46.

4.   Ulman, K.H. (2004). Divided loyalties: Countertransferential pressure associated with combined and conjoint group therapy. *Group,* 28, 227-244.

5.   Weinberg, H. & Ditroi, A. (2007). Concurrent therapy, countertransference and the analytic third. *Group,* 31(1-2), 47-62.

6.   Wong, N. (1983). Combined Individual and group psychotherapy. In H.I. Kaplan & B.J. Sadock (Eds.). *Comprehensive Group Psychotherapy.* Baltimore: Williams and Wilkins.

How and Where to Recruit and Market

Think about and write a list of your best marketing resources and options.

Target referral sources to consider:

- Local networking groups
- Local mental health guild organizations, e.g., California Marriage and Family Therapists, California Psychological Association, etc.
- Physicians
- Local Mental Health Clinic, agencies - intake department's referral list
- Non-profit foundations that serve similar treatment population
- Hospital marketing and intake department referral list
- Local affiliate of the American Group Psychotherapy Association

List 4 other potential referral sources:

1. _____

2. _____

3. _____

4. _____

Directories

For Psychotherapists

☐ American Group Psychotherapy Association's directory listings available to members are provided to the public through their website: wwwAGPA.org

☐ Local affiliates of American Group Psychotherapy Association's directory listings available to members, referrals available to the public

☐ The American Counseling Association's Division of Group Psychotherapists: Association for Specialists in Group Work: www.asgw.org

☐ www.FindGroupTherapy.com

☐ Social Media: LinkedIn groups, etc.

For Para-Professionals

☐ National non-profit organizations with a shared interest in your group's mission

☐ Social Media: LinkedIn etc.

For Writers and Book Group Leaders

☐ National writers organizations directory listings

☐ Local or state writer's groups, book stores, libraries interested in promoting reading

☐ Social Media: LinkedIn, etc.

Distributing your Fliers

The best way to distribute fliers is by hand. Have them with you when you go to professional meetings. When colleagues ask what you are doing, tell them about your groups and offer to give them a flier with more information.

And please, don't plan to spend your precious money on large mailing lists to people who have never heard of you unless you can do so repeatedly with the goal of getting name recognition and eventually some referrals. Mass mailings are not much more effective than cold calling, yielding poor response rates. Begin to think about your colleagues and which ones might be interested in referring some of their patients to your group and start making a list of their contact information.

Fliers - How to Distribute Effectively

- ☐ By hand
- ☐ Snail mail has a low rate of positive return for the cost, unless you have name recognition
- ☐ Email to targeted mailing lists you currently have or purchase
- ☐ Post your flier at mental health training programs, graduate training programs, university and community mental health clinics, non-profit agency bulletin boards, public health clinics, if appropriate

Websites

A website, if attractive, simple and easy to navigate, can be a real asset. It doesn't need to be fancy or long. Straightforward information about your practice, organization, how to contact you, and the types of groups that you run is the crucial information. Your experience and training and/or the purpose of your group, form the core pieces of information most potential patients or group members want to know. In working on your website and when considering using social media to promote your groups, it is important to have a social media policy that is current. Dr. Keely Kolmes has made her social media policy available to clinicians: http://drkkolmes.com/social-media-policy/. And don't forget to include a good professional photograph.

Personal Contacts - Your Best, Low-Cost Marketing Tool

1. Talk it up!
2. Always have your business card with you, easily accessible and distribute freely
3. Keep copies of your flier in your car trunk, ready to be offered to anyone who expresses interest

Tip

Biases against group therapy and the old stigma that it is a second-class form of treatment remain, despite quality research to the contrary. Siegmann (1995) presents compelling information and provides a good overview about its cost effectiveness. For a copy send a reprint request to: Robert M. Siegmann, Quinco Behavioral Health Systems, Box 628, Columbus, IN 47202-0628. Several new articles add quality data supporting the effectiveness of group work. In a recent article, Amy Paturel (2012) in discusses the factors that make group therapy effective.

Les Greene has an article "*Group Therapist as Social Scientist, with Special Reference to the Psychodynamically Oriented Psychotherapist*" published in the September 2012 issue of the American Psychologist. The American Group Psychotherapy's website, www.AGPA.org maintains a section that lists new articles about the efficacy of group work.

The American Psychological Association recently published a resolution on the effectiveness of psychotherapy, including groups, and cited the AGPA Practice Guidelines. This resolution addresses the effectiveness and cost effectiveness of group psychotherapy. The full resolution is available at: http://www.apa.org/news/press/releases/2012/08/resolution-psychotherapy.aspx

Consider sharing the information in these articles when dealing with staff at institutions or agencies, or with therapists who are resistant or fearful of referring to groups. It may also help to reassure potential referral sources that research has shown that group treatment is most effective as an adjunct to individual psychotherapy and that you are open to collaborate with the provider.

Step Two

Plan Implementation

Create a realistic timeline for completing each of the above steps and write the date in your calendar. To avoid getting discouraged, plan to reschedule any target dates that do not get met.

Step Three

Begin screening potential group members. Throughout the group start-up process you may want to refer back to the earlier discussion about screening, screening protocols, and preparation phase in Chapters 4 and 5.

Chapter 10: Termination – The Gold Mine of Group Work

Talking About Termination: Rare Opportunities

The termination phase of group therapy is often the most challenging and rewarding phase of treatment. Group members have the rare opportunity to be fully honest about the wide range of emotions that arise with partings. Most people have never experienced a clear, openly discussed, termination with significant people in their lives.

Termination, like all endings in life is hard for everyone to talk about. In therapy it is one of the most important and overlooked topics. By encouraging open discussion we make rich opportunities possible.

Overview of Different Kinds of Terminations

Examples of "Healthy" Terminations

- Time-limited group ends as planned
- Group member leaves skillfully, with a feeling of accomplishment
- Therapist or co-therapist leaves, processed with reparative effect

Benefits of Healthy Terminations

- Generalizes to outside relationships
- Contributes to reparative learning
- Members learn new ways to deal with and benefit from well-understood endings

Examples of Unhealthy or Traumatic Terminations

Each of these disruptive or traumatic terminations can have long-lasting negative effects on each group member.

- Premature termination of individual group member
- Traumatic termination, e.g., group member fails to return following unfinished/ unresolved conflict between members in prior group session
- Leader unskillfully, asks member to leave group, e.g., no discussion encouraged before or after
- Death of group member, included here since group members can be traumatized if handled unskillfully, or if the leader does not encourage open discussion and create a safe environment for the group to process their reactions
- Therapist or co-therapist leaves, unskillfully handled by leader(s)
- Premature group ending

These less than ideal terminations can be viewed as disruptive, unhealthy, or traumatic. They all risk damage to trust, re-creation of prior trust-traumas, future confidence in group or therapy and help-seeking in general.

For ideas about how to encourage groups to deal openly with termination, see my Termination Agreement and Termination Template, part of my screening and group preparation process on page 59.

A Word About Goodbye Letters from the Group Leader

Group members appreciate my taking the time to write a personalized goodbye letter which I read aloud and give to the member on their last day in group. Many therapists find it daunting to write a one-page letter summarizing the member's progress.

The value of these letters to both the departing member and the group is enormous. Not only is this process therapeutic and valued by group members, it also helps the therapist gain perspective about the work the member has done in group. Furthermore, this crystallizes your thoughts and helps you model how to say goodbye with respect and caring. These letters can be healing when a member leaves prematurely, or is asked by the leader to terminate or to take a leave of absence.

Key Ingredients of a Goodbye Letter

- Summary of the group member's progress, referring to some of their initial goals
- Description of progress made in group
- Remaining issues to be addressed in the future
- Contributions they have made to the group
- Your description and statement of appreciation for the member's progress
- Recommendations for continuation of the work they have done in group, any concerns and wishes for the departing member
- Statement about how you feel about their leaving, for example, "I and the group will miss your renewed sense of humor and willingness to explore tough stuff." "I share the group's concern about the importance of you continuing your twelve step program," etc.
- The therapist's observation of how the individual has handled the termination process

Sample Termination Letters

What follows are templates of two types of farewell latters. The first is a termination letter for use when a group member leaves the group. The second letter is a template to be sent in the event of your temporary unexpected absence. The latter is part of the Therapist's Professional Will system that is described in the next chapter.

Sample Termination Letter to Group Members

Your Letterhead Here

Date: _____

Dear: _____
        (Patient's name)

Congratulations! It has been impressive to witness your successful efforts to talk openly with the group about painful issues from your past and resolve unfinished business that came up in group. As you know, you have made enormous strides in the areas that brought you to group: being able to identify and speak about your feelings, letting others know when you are feeling unseen, handling conflicts without feeling overwhelmed, and allowing the group to see and accept your rebellious side.

[Generalities that feel honest]

I have felt fortunate and honored to be part of the enormous progress you have made during your time in group. You have a lot to be proud of! I know that the group joins me in wishing you all the best.

With warm best wishes,

Signature: _____

Date: _____

Goodbye Letter from a Group Leader

Sample: In the Event of My Unexpected Absence from Clinical Practice

YOUR LETTERHEAD HERE

Date: _____

Dear: _____
       (Patient's name)

You have received this letter because I have become temporarily incapacitated and am unable to call you myself. *<Covering therapist>*, has mailed this letter, using my stationery, in accordance with an agreement we made in *<Year>*. If you are currently in group therapy with me, this letter is to let you know that I am, regretfully, unable at present, <either to continue my psychotherapy practice or keep any further appointments.> *<Covering therapist>*, will be handling my clinical practice in my absence. Please call this therapist for an appointment or for information regarding an appropriate referral. I encourage you to speak with him/her about the emotions that my absence stirs up in you and that you take the time with either this or another therapist to deal with these feelings.

As you probably know, I feel strongly about the importance of allowing adequate time and discussion for patients' feelings about termination and other disruptions of treatment. If it is at all possible, I will make arrangements so that you can do that with me directly. However, if, due to circumstances beyond my control, this is not possible, I hope that you will allow *<Cover therapist>* to assist you in that process.

Depending on the extent and duration of my absence, I may not be available in the future. As I mentioned above, *<Covering therapist>* is handling my practice. This therapist can update you. If you need to be seen before I return to work, he/she can help you find an appropriate therapist.

I have every confidence that *<Covering therapist>* will handle this transition period ethically, competently, and discreetly for us all. Please feel free to contact him/her should you have any questions. *<Covering therapist>* can be reached at ( ) _____.

Very truly yours,

Signature: _____

Date: _____

Chapter 11: The Therapist's Professional Will

A Word About the Therapist's Professional Will

Planning for the Unexpected: Why Every Therapist Needs a Professional Will

Are You in the "It-Won't-Happen-To-Me" Mindset?

It is never too early to plan for the unexpected. We all occasionally get sick or have family emergencies, and eventually we will no longer be able, or wish to continue practicing. The ethical and clinical importance of planning for our temporary and permanent absences is often neglected. Most of us were not taught techniques for skillfully handling expected or unexpected absences. Plus, most clinicians aren't aware that their Ethics Codes require that they have a plan in place for the disposition of their practices in the event of an unplanned absence.

What is the Therapist's Professional Will?

The will is a document detailing your wishes for the continued care of your patients in your absence, whether planned or unplanned, from temporarily losing your voice to serious illness, relocation, retirement, or death. It is designed to reduce the trauma and impact on your patients, colleagues and yourself when you are unavailable. For example, when you have unplanned absences, your professional will addresses the following questions:

- Who has access to your appointment schedule and patient contact information?
- Who will cancel, see on an emergency basis, or make referrals for your patients?
- Who has access to your office keys, voice mail access code, and other details needed in an emergency?
- What will happen to your practice?
- How do you want your patients and their records handled if you are out of commission, either temporarily or permanently?

While the concept of creating a professional will resonates with most helping professionals, the prospect of putting one into place can seem daunting. By making the commitment to work on this important clinical and ethical project, creating a system to handle your practice in your absence, you will gain peace of mind knowing that you have done everything possible to assure continuity of care for your patients.

Being Proactive about Unexpected Absences

The process of creating your own therapist's professional will builds community and eases the stress and burden on your family members, colleagues, and others during a time of crisis. Putting together your own professional will removes the guesswork, confusion and headaches that often accompany any unexpected event in our lives that makes us unavailable to our patients.

The first step is to put together your own "Emergency Response Team," a group of trusted colleagues who will follow your wishes and help you and your patients cope with your unexpected absence. Most of us have someone who covers for us when we go on vacation, so you may already have colleagues who can form the core of your team. One effective strategy is for colleagues to be each other's Emergency Response Team members and agree to meet to help each other develop individualized professional wills.

How about starting now? Take 10 minutes to list 3 colleagues with whom you would be comfortable discussing these ideas and commit to meeting to discuss how you can get started. This will move you one big step closer to creating one of the best gifts you can give your patients, loved ones, and yourself. Completing your own professional will is often a challenging, yet do-able, rewarding and important process. If you are like most therapists, you agree that this is an important project, yet it keeps sliding to the back burner.

The feedback I hear from workshop participants is that it is difficult to get started on one's own. This is why I hired a programmer to design a downloadable system, the *Therapist's Professional Will™ Guidelines for Managing Planned and Unplanned Absence*, described below. It helps to have a buddy plan and a way to keep the motivation up so that you can be like Kyle Doyle, Ph.D., (personal communication, June 2010) who wrote to say she was surprised at how relieved and delighted she was when she finally had her back-up team in place and her professional will completed. Others talk about how difficult it is in the isolation of their private practices to work on their professional will. Taking the first steps towards planning your own back-up system with a few trusted colleagues makes it dramatically easier, even fun!

Did you Know?

The Ethics Codes for
CAMFT
AAMFT
APA (Psychologists)
APA (Psychiatrists)
ACA
NASW

All require that their members make reasonable efforts to ensure continuity of patient services in the event that the therapist's availability is disrupted by: relocation, retirement, illness, disability, or death. Most use similar language to this section from the California Association of Marriage and Family Therapists:

Excerpt:

"Marriage and family therapists are aware of their professional and clinical responsibilities to provide consistent care to patients and do not abandon or neglect patients. Marriage and family therapists, therefore, maintain practices and procedures that assure undisrupted care. Such practices and procedures may include, but are not limited to, providing contact information and specified procedures in case of emergency, or therapist absence, conducting appropriate terminations, and providing for a professional will" (Sec. 1.3).

The Therapist's Professional Will™: Guidelines for Managing Planned and Unplanned Absence Makes it Possible for:

- Your trusted, hand-picked team of professionals to spring into action, contacting your patients, and following your wishes for handling your practice in your absence
- Your patients to get immediate care with minimal disruption in their treatment plan
- Trusted colleagues to confidentially handle your office matters and records in the way you have specified
- Increased freedom for you to focus on your recovery if you are ill or injured, rather than on a disrupted practice
- Your vacations to be truly a time of rest – no more worrying about patients should there be an emergency/crisis

About the Therapist's Professional Will™: Downloadable System

I developed a comprehensive, downloadable system that takes the critical issue of providing therapeutic continuity for patients from concept to practical application. *The Therapist's Professional Will™: Guidelines for Managing Planned and Unplanned Absence* includes the Therapist's Professional Will itself, checklists, templates and forms, and supportive information, to help you make, and document, thoughtful decisions about what's important to you and your patients. Writing your professional will is a lasting gift you can give yourself, your patients, groups, family, and colleagues. To order your own copy of the program, go to the Products page at www.PsychotherapyTools.com.

DISCLAIMER: You are encouraged to work with an attorney in your state before or in conjunction with completing your actual professional will, preferably one familiar with the professional and business needs of mental health providers. This will help you make sure the wishes you spell out in your professional will meet your needs and are compatible with other legal documents you may have already created. You may be advised to also develop an estate plan to protect you and your heirs.

Chapter 12: Closing

Many group psychotherapists and group leaders have created innovative ways to make their groups safe, valuable, and rich experiences. I created this book to share my forms and worksheets and give you an overview of the enormous field of group work.

As Groucho Marx said "We should learn from the mistakes of others. We don't have the time to make them all ourselves."

By addressing the challenging topics of marketing, termination agreements, good-bye letters, and online group agreements, I have attempted to show how planning and preparation help create and sustain groups that thrive.

Yes, groups are high maintenance. They also give the unique gift of connection, understanding, growth, and learning – for members and leaders.

I hope that these materials, references, and resources deepen or renew your appreciation and respect for the healing power of group.

I wish you and your group members all the best on this adventure we call group work.

Chapter 13: Selected References

Agazarian, Y. (2004). System-centered theory for groups. Karnac Books, London.

Agazarian, Y. (2012). Some advantages of applying multidimensional thinking to the teaching, practice, and outcomes of group psychotherapy. *International Journal of Group Psychotherapy*, 33(2), 243-247.

Agazarian, Y. (2012). Systems-centered® group psychotherapy: Putting theory into practice. *International Journal of Group Psychotherapy*, 62(2), 171-195.

AGPA Practice Guidelines for Group Psychotherapy. (2007). Reducing adverse outcomes and the ethical practice of group psychotherapy. (pp. 47-52). NY: American Group Psychotherapy Association.

Amaranto, E.A., & Bender, S.S. (1990). Individual psychotherapy as an adjunct to group psychotherapy. *International Journal of Group Psychotherapy*, 40:91-101.

Barak, A. & Grohol, J.M. (2011). Current and future trends in Internet-supported mental health interventions. *Journal of Technology in Human Services*, 29(3):155-196.

Barak, A., Hen, L., Boniel-Nissim, M., & Shapira, N. (2008). A comprehensive review and a meta-analysis of the effectiveness of internet-based psychotherapeutic interventions. *Journal of Technology in Human Services*, 26:109-160.

Beck, A.P. (1981). Developmental characteristics of the system-forming process. In Durkin J.E. (Ed.) Living Groups: Group Psychotherapy and General System Theory. NY: Bruner/Mazel, Inc.

Bellman, G. & Ryan, K. (2011). Extraordinary groups: How ordinary teams achieve amazing results. San Francisco, CA: Jossey-Bass.

Bieling, P., McCabe, R., & Anthony, M. (Eds.). (2006). Cognitive-behavioral therapy in groups. NY: Guilford Press.

Bernard, H.S. (1989). Guidelines to minimize premature terminations. *International Journal of Group Psychotherapy*, 39, 523-529.

Bernard, H., Burlingame, G., Flores, P., Greene, L, Joyce, A., Kobos, J., & Feirman, D. (2008). Clinical practice guidelines for group psychotherapy. *International Journal of Group Psychotherapy*, 58(4), 455-542.

Bieling, P., McCabe, R., & Anthony, M. (Eds.). (2006). Cognitive-behavioral therapy in groups. NY: Guilford Press.

Billow, R. (2002). Passion in group: Thinking about loving, hating, and knowing. *International Journal of Group Psychotherapy*, 52(3), 455-542.

Billow, R. (2001). The therapist's anxiety and resistance to group therapy. *International Journal of Group Psychotherapy*, 51(2), 225-242.

Billow, R.M. (2010). On Resistance. *International Journal of Group Psychotherapy*, 60(3):313-346.

Billow, R.M. (2006). The three R's of group: Resistance, rebellion, and refusal. *International Journal of Group*, 56(3), 259-284.

Bion, F. (1995). The days of our lives. *The Institute of Psychoanalysis*. Retrieved from http://www.psychoanalysis.org.uk/days.htm.

Brabender, V. (2006). The ethical group psycotherapist. *International Journal of Group Psychotherapy*, 56(4), 395-413.

Brabender, V. & Fallon, A. (2009). Ethical hot spots of combined individual and group therapy: Applying four ethical systems. *International Journal of Group Psychotherapy*, 59(1):127-147.

Brown, N.W. (2004). Psychoeducational groups: Process and practice. NY: Brunner-Routledge.

Brown, N. (2011). Psychoeducational groups. NY: Routledge. Personal correspondence August 25, 2014.

Brown, N. (2014). Facilitating challenging groups, leaderless, open, and single session groups. NY: Routledge Taylor & Francis Group.

Buckinghame, D. & Willett, R. (2006). Digital generations: Children, young people and new media. Lawrence Erlbaum Associates, Publishers.

Budman, S. & Gurman, A. (1994). *Theory and practice of brief psychotherapy*. NY: Guilford Press.

Butler, L.D., Koopman, C., Neri, E., Giese-Davis, J., Palesh, O., Thorne-Yocam, K.A., Dimiceli, S., Chen, X., Fobair, P., Kraemer, H.C., Spiegel, D. (2009). Effects of supportive-expressive group therapy on pain in women with metastatic breast cancer. *Health Psychology*, *28*(5), 579-587.

Caffaro, J.V., Conn-Caffaro, C., Sibling Dynamics, & Group Psychotherapy. (April 2003). *International Journal of Group Psychotherapy*, 53, 125-154.

Cerel, J., Padgett, J.H., & Reed, R.A. (2009). Support groups for suicide survivors: Results of a survey of group leaders. *Suicide and Life-Threatening Behavior*, 39(6):588-598.

Classen, C.C. & Spiegel, D. (2011). Supportive-expressive group psychotherapy, in handbook of psychotherapy in cancer care (eds M. Watson and D.W. Kissane), John Wiley & Sons, Ltd., Chichester, UK.

Cohen, B.D. (2002). Group to resolve conflicts between groups: Diplomacy with a therapeutic dimension. *Group*, 26(3):189-204.

Comas-Diaz, L. & Jacobsen, F. (1991). Ethnocultural transference and countertransference in the therapeutic dyad. *American Journal of Orthopsychiatry*, 61, 392-403.

Comstock, B.S., & McDermott, M. (1975). Group therapy for patients who attempt suicide. *International Journal of Group Psychotherapy*, 25, 44-49.

Corde, B., Cornwall, T., & Whiteside, R. (1984). Increasing effectiveness of co-therapy. *International Journal of Group Psychotherapy*, 34, 643-654.

Counselman, E.F. & Weber, R. (2002). Changing the guard: New leadership for an established group. *International Journal of Group Psychotherapy*, 52(3) 373-386.

Crosby, G. & Altman, D. (2012). Integrative cognitive-behavioral group therapy. In J. Kleinberg (Ed.), Handbook of Group Psychotherapy. Hoboken, NJ: Wiley Press.

Cunningham, J.M. & Knight, E. (1996). Mothers, models and mentors: Issues in long-term group therapy for women. In B. DeChant (Ed.), *Women and Group Psychotherapy Theory and Practice* (pp. 284-299). NY: Guilford Press.

DeLucia-Waack, J., Kalodner, C.R. & Riva, M.T. (Eds.). (2014). The handbook of group counseling and psychotherapy, Los Angeles, CA: Sage Publications.

Doyle, K. (2010). Personal communication.

Drumm, D.J. & Knott, E.J. (2009). Theme groups at thirty. *International Journal of Group Psychotherapy*, October, 59:4:491-510.

Dugo, J.M. & Beck, A.P.A. (1984). A therapist's guide to issues of intimacy and hostility viewed as group-level phenomenon. *International Journal of Group Psychotherapy*, 34(1), 25-47.

Dugo, J.M. & Beck, A.P.A. (1997). Significance and complexity of early phases in the development of the co-therapy relationship. *Group Dynamics: Theory, Research, and Practice, 1*(4), 294-304.

Eskin, V. (2010). Ladies in waiting: A group intervention for families coping with deployed soldiers. *International Journal of Group Psychotherapy*, 61(3):414-437.

Fieldsteel, N.D. (1996). When the therapist says goodbye. *International Journal of Group Psychotherapy*, 55(2), 245-279.

Foulkes, S.H. (1961). Group process and the individual in the therapeutic group. *British Journal of Medical Psychology*, 34:23-31.

Foulkes, S.H. & Anthony, E.J. (1965). Group psychotherapy, the psychoanalytic approach. Karnac Books, London.

Foulkes, S.H. (1986). Group analytic psychotherapy: Method and principles. Karnac Books, London.

Gans, J. (1990). Broaching and exploring the question of combined group and individual therapy. *International Journal of Group Psychotherapy*, 40, 123-137.

Gans, J. (1989). Hostility in group psychotherapy. *International Journal of Group Psychotherapy*, 39, 499-515.

Gans, J. & Alonso, A. (1998). Difficult patients: Their construction in group therapy. *International Journal of Group Psychotherapy*, 48(3), 311-345.

Gans, J. & Counselman, E. (2010). Patient selection for psychodynamic group psychotherapy: practical and dynamic considerations. *International Journal of Group Psychotherapy*, 60(2), 197-220.

Gans. J. (1992). Money and psychodynamic group psychotherapy. *International Journal of Group Psychotherapy*, 42(1), 133-152.

Gans, J. & Shapiro, E. (2008). The courage of the group therapist. *International Journal of Group Psychotherapy*, 58(3), 345-361.

Gans, J. & Counselman, E. (2010). Patient selection for psychodynamic group psychotherapy: Practiceal and dynamic considerations. International Journal of Group Psychotherapy, 60(2), 196-220.

Gantt, S.P. (2013). Applying systems-centered theory (SCT) and methods in organizational contexts: Putting SCT to work. *International Journal of Group Psychotherapy*, 63(2), 234-258

Gantt , S.P. & Badenoch, B. (2013). The interpersonal neurobiology of group psychotherapy and group process. Karnac Books, London.

Gold, J. (December 24, 2013). Personal communication.

Greene. L. (2012). Group therapist as social scientist, with special reference to the psychodynamically oriented psychotherapist. *American Psychologist*, 67(6), 477-489.

Greene, L.R. (2012). Studying the how and why of therapeutic change: The increasingly prominent role of mediators in group psychotherapy research. *International Journal of Group Psychotherapy*, 62(2):325-331.

Gross, J. (2014). (Personal correspondence Joshua M. Gross, Ph.D., ABPP, CGP, FAGPA and Anne M. Slocum McEneaney, Ph.D., ABPP, CGP, FAGPA, August 12, 2014).

HarPaz, N. (1994). Failures in group psychotherapy: The therapist variable. *International Journal of Group Psychotherapy*, 44(1), 3-21.

Hoffman, L. *Preparing the Patient for Group Psychotherapy*, Price, J.R., Hescheles, D.R., Price, Rae, A. (1999) (eds.) *A Guide to Starting Psychotherapy Groups,* Academic Press, London. pp. 25-43.

Hopper, E. (2005). Countertransference in the context of the fourth basic assumption in the unconscious life of groups. *International Journal of Group Psychotherapy*, 55(1):87-113.

Hughes, M., Patterson, L.B., & Terrell, J.B. (2005). Emotional intelligence in action: Training and coaching activities for leaders, managers, and teams; San Francisco, CA: Pfeiffer.

Joffe, P. (2008). An empirically supported program to prevent suicide in a college student population. *Suicide and Life-Threatening Behavior*, 38(1):87-103.

Johnson, D. & Johnson, F. (2013). Joining together (11th ed). Upper Saddle River NJ: Pearson.

Kauff, P.F. (2009). Transference in combined individual and group psychotherapy. *International Journal of Group Psychotherapy*, 59:29-46.

Kauff, P.F. (1977). The germination process: Its relationship to the separation–individuation phase of development. *International Journal of Group Psychotherapy*, 27:3-18.

Kauth, B. (1992). A circle of men: The original manual for men's support groups. St. Martin's Press, NY.

Kira, I.A., Ahmed, A., Wasim, F., Mahmoud, V., Colrain, J., & Rai, D. (2012). Group therapy for refugees and torture survivors: Treatment model innovations. *International Journal of Group Psychotherapy*, 62(1):69-88.

Kleinberg, J. (Ed.). (2011). The Wiley-Blackwell Handbook of Group Psychotherapy, John Wiley & Sons, Ltd., Chichester, UK.

Knauss, L.K. (2006). Ethical issues in record keeping in group psychotherapy. *International Journal of Group Psychotherapy*, 56:415-430.

Kolmes, K., Merz Nagel, D., & Anthony, K. (2012). Ethical framework for the use of social media by mental health professionals. Online Therapy Institute.

Kozlowski, K.A. & Holmes, C.M. (2014). Experiences in online process groups: A qualitative study. *The Journal for Specialists in Group Work,* 39(4):276-300.

Kraut, R., Patterson, M., Lundmark, V., Kiesler, S., Mukopadhyay, T., & Scherlis, W. (1998). Internet paradox: A social technology that reduces social involvement and psychological well-being. *American Psychologist*, 53(9):1017-1031.

Kurz, L.F. (1990a). The self-help movement: Review of the past decade of research. *Social Work With Groups,* 13(3):104-112.

Layton, L. (2006). Racial identities, racial enactments, and normative unconscious processes. *Psychoanalytic Quarterly,* 75(2):237-269.

Leicht, C., Crisp, R.J., & Randsley de Moura, G. (2013). Need for structure predicts leadership preference. *Group Dynamics, Theory, Research, and Practice*, 17(1):53-66.

Liebert, T.W., Smith-Adcock, S., & Munson, J. (2008). Exploring how online self-help groups compares to face-to-face groups from the user perspective. *Journal of Technology in Counseling*, 5(1) Retrieved 30 December 2012 from jtc.columbusstate.edu/Vol5_1/Liebert.htm.

Lieberman, M.A. (1990). A group therapist perspective on self-help groups. *International Journal of Group Psychotherapy,* 40(3):251-278.

Lieberman, M.A. & Borman, L.D. (1979). Self-help groups for coping with crisis: Origins members, processes, and impact. San Francisco: Jossey-Bass.

Lieberman, M., Golant, M., & Altman, T. (2004). Therapeutic norms and patient benefit: Cancer patients in professionally directed support. *Group Dynamics: Theory, Research, and Practice,* 8(4):265-276.

Lieberman, M.A. & Whittaker, D.M. (2008). Psychotherapeutic change through the group process. NY: Aldine Transaction.

Livingstone, L.R. (2006). No place to hide: The group leader's moments of shame. *International Journal of Group Psychotherapy,* 56(3):307- 323.

Livingstone, S., Haddon, L. Gorzig, A., & Olafsson, K. (2011). Risks and safety on the internet: The perspective of European children. LSE, London: EU Kids Online: www.eukidsonline.net.

MacKensie, K.R. (1997). Time-managed group psychotherapy: Effective clinical applications. Washington, DC: American Psychiatric Press.

MacKenzie, R. (1990). Introduction to time limited group psychotherapy. American Psychiatric Press, Washington, D.C.

Mangione, L., Rosalind F.R., & Iacuzzi, C.M. (2007). Ethics and endings in group psychotherapy: Saying good-bye and saying it well. *International Journal of Group Psychotherapy,* 57(1):25-40.

Maramosh, C., Holtz, A., & Schottenbauer, M. (2005). Group cohesiveness, group-derived collective self-esteem, group-derived hope, and the well-being of group therapy members. *Group Dynamics: Theory, Research, and Practice,* 9(1):32-24.

McFarlane, W. (2002). Multifamily groups in the treatment of severe psychiatric disorders. NY: The Guilford Press.

Motherwell, L. (2011). Support and process-oriented therapy groups. The Wiley-Blackwell Handbook of Group Psychotherapy, John Wiley & Sons, Ltd., Chichester, UK, 275-298.

Motherwell, L. (2002). Women, money and psychodynamic group therapy. *International Journal of Group Psychotherapy,* 52(1):49-66.

Motherwell, L., Shay, J.J. (2014). Complex dilemmas in group therapy: Pathways to resolution. NY: Routledge.

Napier, R.W. & Gershenfeld, M.K. (2003). Groups: Theory and experience (4th ed). Boston, MA: Houghton Miflin.

Novick, J. (1997). Termination conceivable and inconceivable. *Psychoanalytic Psychology,* 14:145-162.

Ogrodniczuk, J., Piper, W., McCallum, M., Joyce, A., & Rosie, J.S. (2002). Interpersonal predictors of group therapy outcome for complicated grief. *International Journal of Group Psychotherapy*, 52(4):511-535.

O'Neill, S. & Kueppenbender, K. (2012). Suicide in group therapy: Trauma and possibility. *International Journal of Group Psychotherapy*, (62)4:586-611.

Ormont, L. (1993). Resolving resistances to immediacy in the group setting. *International Journal of Group Psychotherapy*, 43:399-419.

Ormont, L. (1969). Group resistance and the therapeutic contract. *International Journal of Group Psychotherapy*, 18:147-154.

Ormont, L. (1990). The craft of bridging. *International Journal of Group Psychotherapy*, 40:3-17.

Paturel, A. (2012). Power in numbers: Research is pinpointing the factors that make group therapy successful. *American Psychological Association's Monitor*. 43(10):48-49.

Peleg, I. (2012). Oppression, freedom, and recognition in an analytic therapy group: Group and therapist interactions from relational and group analytic perspectives. *International Journal of Group Psychotherapy*, 62(3):437-458.

Perron, B. (2002). Online support group for caregivers of people with a mental illness. *Psychiatric Rehabilitation Journal*, 26:70-71

Phillips, S. & Kane, D. (2008). Healing together after trauma: A couple's guide to coping with trauma and post-traumatic stress. Oakland CA: New Harbinger Publications. Retrieved from www.couplesaftertrauma.com; http://blogs.psychcentral.com/healing-together/.

Phillips, S.B. (2014). The dangerous role of silence in the relationship between trauma and violence: A group response. *International Journal of Group Psychotherapy*, 65:1:64-87.

Piper, W.E. & McCallum, M. (1994). Selection of patients for group interventions. In H.S. Bernard and K.R. Mackenzie (Eds.). Basics of Group Psychotherapy (pp. 1-34). NY: Guilford.

Piper, W.E., McCallum, M., & Azim H.F.A. (1992). Adaptation to loss through short term psychotherapy. NY: Guilford.

Poey, K. (1985). Guidelines for brief, dynamic group therapy. *International Journal of Group Psychotherapy*, 35(3):331-351.

Polak, M. (2006). It's a url thing: community versus commodity in girl-focused netscape. In: D Buckingham & R.W. Mahwah (Eds.), Digital Generations: Children, Young People and New Media (pp.177-1973). NJ and London: Lawrence Erlbaum.

Price, J.R., Hescheles, D.R., & Price, Rae, A. (1999) (eds.). *A Guide to Starting Psychotherapy Groups,* Academic Press, London.

Reynolds, D.J. Jr., Stiles, W.B., & Grohol, J.M. (2006). An investigation of session impact and alliance in internet based psychotherapy: Preliminary results. *Counseling and Psychotherapy Research*, 6:164-168

Rice, C., Shapiro, E., & Shay, J. (2011). Death of a group therapist and the survival of the group. *International Journal of Group Psychotherapy Association*, 61(2):178-183.

Ridley, C.R. (2005). Overcoming unintentional racism in counseling and therapy: A practitioner's guide to intentional intervention (2nd Ed.). Thousand Oaks, CA: SAGE.

Rioch, M.J. (1970). The work of Wilfred Bion on groups. *Psychiatry,* (33)1:56-66.

Roth, D. & Covi, L. (1984). Cognitive group psychotherapy of depression: The open-ended group. *International Journal of Group Psychotherapy*, 34(1):67-82.

Rutan, J.S., Stone, W.N., & Shay J. (2014). Psychodynamic Group Psychotherapy (5th ed). NY: Guilford.

Schafer, R. (1973). The termination of brief psychoanalytic psychotherapy. *International Journal of Group Psychotherapy,* 11:135-148.

Seligman, M. (1995). The effectiveness of psychotherapy. *Consumer Reports*, 50(12):965-974.

Schermer, V. (2009). On the vicissitudes of combining individual and group psychotherapy. *The International Journal of Group Psychotherapy*, 59(1):149-162.

Schloper Galinksy (1995) Expanding our view of support groups as open systems. *Social Work With Groups,* 18(1):3-10.

Shapiro, E. & Ginzberg, R. (2002). Parting gifts: Termination rituals in group therapy. *International Journal of Group Psychotherapy*, 52(3):319-336.

Shapiro, E. & Ginzberg, R. (2006). Buried treasure: Money, ethics and countertransference in group psychotherapy. *The International Journal of Group Psychotherapy*, 56(4):477-494.

Shechtman, Z. & Rybko, J. (2004). Attachment style and observed initial self-disclosure as explanatory variables of group functioning. *Group Dynamics: Theory, Research, and Practice.* 8(3): 207-220.

Siegmann, R. & Long, G. (1995). Psychoeducational group therapy changes the face of managed care. *Journal of Practice Psychology and Behavioral Health*, 29-36.

Simon, J. (1992). The group therapist's absence and the substitute leader. *The International Journal of Group Psychotherapy*, 42(2):287-291.

Spiegel, D. & Classen, C. (2000). Group therapy for cancer patients: A research-based handbook of psychosocial care. Basic Books, NY.

Steiner, A. (2001). When the therapist has to cancel. *The California Therapist*, 52-54.

Steiner, A. (2004). The therapist protection plan: Preparing for expected and unexpected absences from practice. *The California Therapist*, 22-29.

Steiner, A. (2007). The empty chair: Making therapist absences less traumatic for everyone. *The New Therapist*, 48:11-21.

Steiner, A. (2011). The therapist's professional will: A backup plan every clinician needs. *Group Special Issue: The Aging of Group Therapists*, 35(1):33-39.

Steiner, A. (2011). Therapists need a strong back-up plan. *The National Psychologist*, 20-21.

Steiner, A. (2014). The therapist's professional will: If not now, when? *The Therapist*, 22-29.

Sue, D. (2010). Microaggressions in everyday life: Race, gender and sexual orientation. Hobroken, NY:Wiley Publishing.

Toseland R.W. & Siporin, M. (1986). When to recommend group treatment: A review of the clinical and group literature. *International Journal of Group Psychotherapy*, 36:171-201.

Tuckman, B.W. & Jensen, M.A. (1977). Stages of small-group development revisited. *Group Org. Studies,* 2:419-27.

Tuckman, B.W. (1965). Developmental sequence in small groups. *Psychological Bulletin*, 63:384-399.

Turkle, S. (2011). Alone together: Why we expect more from technology and less from each other. NY: Basic Books.

Ulman, K. (2001). Unwitting exposure of the therapist: Transferential and countertransferential dilemmas. *Journal of Psychotherapy Practice Research*, 10(1):14-22.

Ulman, K.H. (2004). Divided loyalties: Countertransferential pressure associated with combined and conjoint group therapy. *Group,* 28:227-244.

Ulman, K.H. (2004). Group interventions for treatment of trauma in adults. In B.J. Buchele & H.I. Spitz (Eds.). *Group Interventions for Treatment of Psychological Trauma.* NY: AGPA

Vacha-Haase, T., Ness, C., Dannison, L., & Smith, A. (2000). Grandparents raising grandchildren: A psychoeducational group approach. *Journal for Specialists in Group Work,* 25(1): 67-78.

Violette, B.L. (2012). Group process and problems in psychoanalytic education. *Contemporary Psychoanalysis*, Vol. 48, No. 4. NY: William Alanson White Institute.

Viverito, K.M., Cardin, S.A., Johnson, L.A., & Owen, R.R. (2013). Lessons learned from two peer-led mutual support groups. *International Journal of Group Psychotherapy*, 63(4):593-608.

von Bertalanffy, L. (1969). General system theory: Foundations, development, applications. NY: George Braziller Inc.

von Bertalanffy, L. (1966). General system theory, and psychiatry. In S. Ariete (Ed.), American Handbook of Psychiatry, NY: Basic Books. 705-721.

Walker, L.M., Bischoff, T.F., Robinson, J.W. (2010). Supportive expressive group therapy for women with advanced ovarian cancer. *International Journal of Group Psychotherapy,* 60(3):407-427.

Weber, R.L. & Gans, J. (2003). The group therapist's shame: A much undiscussed topic. *International Journal of Group Psychotherapy*, 53(4):395-417.

Weber, R.L. (2006). Principles of group psychotherapy. NY: American Group Psychotherapy Association, Inc. (AGPA website, or telephone: 888-808-2472).

Weinberg, H. (2014). The paradox of internet groups: Alone in the presence of virtual others. Karnac Books, London.

Weinberg H. & Ditroi, A. (2007). Concurrent therapy, countertransference and the analytic third. *Group*, 31(1-2):47-62.

Weinberg H., Nuttman-Shwartz O., & Gilmore, M. (2005). Trauma groups: An overview. *Group Analysis*, 38(2):189-204.

Weinberg H. & Schneider S. (2003). Introduction: Background, structure and dynamics of the large group. In S. Schneider & H. Weinberg (eds.). The Large Group Revisited: *The Herd, Primal Horde, Crowds and Masses.* Jessica Kingsley, London.

Weiner, M.F. (1978). Therapist disclosure: The use of self in psychotherapy. Butterworths, London.

Wender, L. (1964). The dynamics of group psychotherapy and its application. *Journal of Nervous and Mental Disease*, 84:54-60.

Whitman-Raymond, M.M. (2009). The influence of class in the therapeutic dyad. *Contemporary Psychoanalysis,* 45:429-443.

Wilson, D. (2010). Reducing isolation: An adult cystic fibrosis support group sponsored by the University of Wisconsin Pulmonary and Critical Care Medicine. Retrieved from http://videos.med.wisc.edu/videos/1149.

Wong, N. (1983). Combined individual and group psychotherapy. In H.I. Kaplan & B.J. Sadock (Eds.). *Comprehensive Group Psychotherapy.* Baltimore:Williams and Wilkins.

Wurst, F.M., Kunz, I., Skipper, G., Wolfersdorf, M., Beine, K.H., Vogel, R., Müller, S., & Petitjean, Thon, N. (2013). How therapists react to patient's suicide: findings and consequences for health care professionals' wellbeing. *General Hospital Psychiatry,* 35:565-570

Yalom, I.D. & Leszcz, M. (2005). The Theory and Practice of Group Psychotherapy (5th ed). NY: Basic Books.

Online Resource

Keely Kolmes' website provides a free resource: Social media policies for therapists: Retrieve from http://drkkolmes.com/for-clinicians/social-media-policy/.

Selected Major Group Therapy Organizations/Resources

The American Group Psychotherapy Association publishes the *International Journal of Group Psychotherapy*, NY: The Guilford Press. Retrieve from www.AGPA.org.

The Association for Specialists in Group Work, part of the American Counseling Association, publishes the *Journal for Specialists in Group* London:Sage Publications. Retrieve from http://www.asgw.org/.

The International Association for Group Psychotherapy and Group Processes, IAGP runs international congresses and publishes Forum. Retrieve from www.iagp.com.

International Association for the Advancement of Social Work with Groups, Inc. (AASWG) affiliated with these publications. *Social work with groups - A journal of community and clinical practice and groupwork*, and g*roupwork*. Retrieve from www.aaswg.org.

The Canadian Group Psychotherapy Association (www.cgpa.ca); The Group-Analytic Society's journal *Group Analysis*, published by Sage Publications, London. Retrieve from http://gaq.sagepub.com.

If you want to learn more about leading therapy groups, you will find networking and learning opportunities by joining your local affiliate of the American Group Psychotherapy Association. By attending their sponsored workshops you can get credits to become a Certified Group Psychotherapist, part of the National Registry of Group Psychotherapists. In addition to reduced rates at conferences and training events, membership in the American Group Psychotherapy Association gives you free online access to the *International Journal of Group Psychotherapy*, an invaluable resource for learning more about any type and aspect of group work. For the most up-to-date information regarding these, and other group therapy training and referral resources, and other resources please see the Resources and Links page at www.PsychotherapyTools.com.

Note: *The world of group work, although constantly expanding through the Internet, has countless resources. From helpful advice and practical tips for working with cross-cultural groups, to traditional long-term psychodynamic psychotherapy groups, this list includes some of my favorite resources that address frequently asked questions. It is not intended to be an exhaustive review of the literature. Rather, you may use it as a starting point for a lifelong process of finding new resources.*

Postscript

Congratulations on investing in making your groups healthier and reducing unnecessary stress for you and your groups!

Now you can concentrate on having fun leading your groups.

Enjoy!

Ann Steiner, Ph.D.
Ann Steiner, Ph.D., MFT, CGP, FAGPA

About The Author

Ann Steiner, Ph.D. is passionate about the healing power of group work.

Her dedication to making groups safer for members dates back to the 1980's when she was in the vanguard, providing free clinical consultation to self-help groups.

She is a Certified Group Psychotherapist and Licensed Marriage and Family Therapist in the San Francisco Bay Area, leading groups for 30 years.

Dr. Steiner is a faculty member of The Psychotherapy Institute's Group Therapy Training Program and served as an Associate Clinical Professor at the University of California Medical School, San Francisco.

She is a Board member and Fellow of the American Group Psychotherapy Association, past president of Northern California Group Psychotherapy Society, and a founding member of the National Registry of Group Psychotherapists.

In addition to being a frequent chapter contributor and professional speaker, Dr. Steiner has published over 20 articles about her pioneering work on the therapist's professional will. Her innovative work led her to create and develop a downloadable system, The Therapist's Professional Will™: Guidelines for Managing Planned and Unplanned Absence and her free Medical Information Form, an easy-to-use, updatable computer record of medications and emergency information, www.DrSteiner.com.

Currently she is completing a version of this book for non-therapists who lead groups, such as writer's groups, work groups, community and networking groups, etc. She is also writing a self-help book about dealing with chronic medical illness. For more information designed for therapists, see: www.PsychotherapyTools.com. Her public website is: www.DrSteiner.com. She can be contacted directly at info@PlanAheadPress.

Made in the USA
Coppell, TX
05 September 2020